SUNSCREEN LOVE

sunscreen
LOVE

The 4 Phases
to Find The Love You Want

COACH RATNER

Book cover & interior design by:

Joanna & Grzegorz Japoł - LUNA Design Studio

Other Books
by Coach Ratner

*Never Feel Unloved Again: Symptoms & Strategies
to Cure Low Self-Esteem*

Score: Mastering Wisdom, Wealth and Happiness

Find Your Awesome

The 10 Secrets to Find the Love of Your Life

The 10 Secrets to a Passionate Marriage

All of my books are available on Amazon,
with many offered as free downloads at
CoachRatner.com.
You can also enjoy select titles as audiobooks
for no charge on my podcast.

Podcast

The Coach Ratner Podcast

Live Events

Want to inspire your company, organization, or
school? Bring Coach Ratner and transform your next
live event! Contact me at **CoachRatner@gmail.com**

Sample Classes

Relationships

Sunscreen Love

The Emotional Vampire

Beaming Self-Esteem

Raising Superstars

The 10 Commandments of Marriage

From Swim Right to Wedding Night:
Make Yourself Irresistibly Marriageable

Leadership & Business Development

3 Secrets to Success

3 Steps to Powerful Public Speaking

The Art of Persuasion;
How to Get What You Want in Life

From the Western Wall to Wall Street:
Building Organizations for Success

Motivation & Personal Development

The Lamb & Lamborghini

Body, Soul, or Poke Bowl

Be a Joy Jew, Not an Oy Jew

4 Steps to Your Personal Redemption

Ignite Your Greatness:
What I Learned From Losing a Lung

Table of Contents

Start Here 9

Phase 1 - The Crush **17**

To Catch the Right Fish,
You Need the Right Bait 18

Clarify Why You are Dating 21

Date Them, Don't Mate Them 26

The Three Date Rule 31

Beware of the New Face Factor 35

The Feeling of Being in Love 40

Defining Love 43

Chopped: Fire Up Your Relationship! 45

Square Peg Into Round Hole 47

You Don't Know Your Type…
Until You Meet Your Type 50

The Soulmate Discovery Worksheet 55

Phase 2 - The Research **57**

Learning to Listen 59

Read the Back of Your Shirt 65

Your Ego is Not Your Amigo 71

You Must Love Yourself 75

Defining Marriage 78

The Three Questions You Must Ask
Before Getting Married 83

Body, Soul or Poke Bowl 101

Phase 3 - The Commitment **110**

Sunscreen Love 111

Compliment, Don't Criticize 116

The 4 A's: Attention, Affection,
Appreciation & Awareness 119

A Monthly Honeymoon 137

Infinite Marriage 145

When Divorce is Necessary 154

Phase 4 - Never Leaving **160**

What's Important to You Is Important to Me 161

Sometimes You Have to be Wrong to be Right ... 166

The 24 Hour Rule 169

Don't Let Politics Trump Your Marriage 174

Think Before You Speak 177

SLIM: Sometimes Less is More 182

Final Blessing 185

About The Author 187

**Preview For: Never Feel Unloved Again:
Symptoms & Strategies To Cure
Low Self-Esteem** **189**

Start Here 190

The Symptoms of Low Self-Esteem 195

Start Here

**In the morning
I found her sleeping on my front porch.**

A few hours later, I was on the phone with the county police, trying to prevent a tragic suicide attempt on the side of the highway. This came after days of her relentless calls—every 30 seconds, day after day.

She used my hide-a-key to let herself into my house, rummaged through my home office, and wrote a $20,000 check to herself from my checkbook. She left it on my desk, almost as if she wanted me to find it. I don't think she ever intended to steal the money. The check was her way of telling me she was unraveling mentally. And that might be putting it mildly.

I hesitantly walked into my bedroom, half-expected to find a severed horse's head on my pillow.

This is what happens when you can't define love.

The breakup came after just two months of dating. I knew I was a good catch, but not one worth dying for. I know what it feels like to be dumped—it's a constant, gnawing ache in your gut, and the only remedy is time. Emotions aren't something you can quantify or display for others to understand; they're internal, and only you truly know how deeply the pain hurts. You can't pass that feeling onto someone else. That's why there's no such thing as an easy breakup. However, the pain of a divorce will be exponentially worse than any short-lived relationship.

When the relationship does not go as you had dreamed, it feels like the world is crumbling around you.

At our core, we all strive for the same thing, whether we're fully aware of it or it's buried deep within us: a loving, passionate relationship that lasts a lifetime. I genuinely believe that everyone reading this book has a real chance to achieve that. But the truth is, only a few will reach that point. It takes mental discipline, the ability to control your emotions, and the willingness to be vulnerable and let someone into your heart.

Being in love means two people opening up to one another, sharing their thoughts and feelings, and, more importantly, being emotionally open for each other.

When we're young, love isn't something we think much about. But by our late teens, the idea of dating starts to become a reality. Have you ever heard of anyone taking a class on dating and marriage before diving in? Probably not. Most people approach it through trial and error, hoping for the best. But when it comes to making one of the most important decisions of your life, would you really want to rely on hope and luck? That sounds almost insane.

Much of what we know from marriage comes from what we experienced growing up in our homes. If our parents had a healthy marriage, then we have something good to emulate. If not, we might need to put in more effort to cultivate a healthy relationship of our own.

Another place we get an idea of what marriage is supposed to look like is from romantic comedies and Disney movies. Unfortunately, movies give us a misleading sense of what marriage truly is. Think about it—what's usually the final scene in a romantic comedy? The wedding. Why don't they ever show the couple 20, 30, or even 40 years after the wedding? Because it wouldn't be a romantic comedy, it would be a murder mystery! The reality is, Prince Charming isn't going to magically fix everything in your life, despite what these stories suggest. If you're always holding out for the "perfect" prince or princess, you might never commit, constantly believing that ideal person is just around the corner. This mindset could be why people are marrying later in life, or sometimes not at all.

Has access to internet dating increased your chances of finding love? Maybe, maybe not. The ease of access to endless options can make people more selective—quick to dismiss someone for being a few pounds overweight or having a tiny pimple on their nose. With so many alternatives just a swipe away, it's tempting to find any small excuse to keep searching, even when you've met someone who could lead to a deep, passionate relationship.

We may falsely believe that having multiple dating options actually makes it easier to choose one that we're truly happy with. In reality though, the abundance of options actually requires more effort to make a decision and can easily leave us feeling less satisfied with what we choose. This phenomenon is known as the Paradox of Choice.

It's kind of like going to a restaurant with an overwhelming menu–how many times have you ordered the chicken marsala, only to immediately regret not trying the salmon teriyaki? In theory, you love the large menu, but then you are never satisfied with what you ordered because there were so many other good choices. This is why it is called a paradox.

This concept was popularized by American psychologist Barry Schwartz.[1] Schwartz has long studied the ways in which economics and psychology intersect. He became interested in seeing the way that choices were affecting the happiness of citizens in Western societies. He found that while we have far more options than people did in the past, consumer satisfaction hasn't increased as much as traditional economic theories would predict.

Marriage rates in the U.S. have steadily declined since the early 1970s. The peak occurred in 1946, with over 16 marriages per year per 1,000 people. By 1973, that number had dropped to 11, and today it sits below 7 marriages per 1,000 people annually.

Dating used to be simpler: if you met someone nice with a steady job, you married them. Today's singles are less inclined to settle for someone they would have considered a good match in the past.

This is why understanding the different stages of love is essential—not only for having a more fulfilling relationship, but also for making it easier to find love in the first place. Will reading this book guarantee that you'll find love? No, but it will guarantee that if you're open to learning the 4 Phases of Love and allow yourself to be vulnerable, you will significantly increase your chances of finding a meaningful connection.

It's just like anything else in life—if you don't know the steps, you're more likely to give up. Imagine taking a yoga class for the first time, and the instructor only teaches you how to do downward dog. Technically, you know a yoga pose, but without learning the variety of poses, your practice will never truly develop, and whatever joy

---

1   The Paradox of Choice: Why More is Less. Ecco Publishers

you initially had for it will eventually fade. The same applies to relationships. If we don't understand the phases necessary to cultivate true love, we risk falling out of love with our partner or spouse, ultimately becoming another failed statistic.

We often believe we understand love and can succeed at it with the knowledge we have. Yet, as marriage and divorce statistics show, it's far more challenging than we realize. No couple walks down the aisle expecting to become part of those statistics. Don't leave the success of your relationship to chance—take control of building the love you truly desire.

In the Western world, the divorce rate hovers between 50% and 60%. However, consider the marriages that don't end in divorce—how many of those couples would describe themselves as being in a happy, passionate relationship? Let's say it's around 50%, which is probably generous. This means that if you're currently in a relationship, whether married or not, your chances of enjoying a lasting, passionate, and fulfilling connection are less than 25%. These statistics are disheartening, and this book is dedicated to helping change that.

We will break down love into four distinct phases. Understanding each phase will assist you in the ongoing development of your relationship. Once you've completed one phase, you'll shift your focus to the next, guiding you through the journey and helping you avoid the critical mistake of marrying the wrong person or staying in a toxic relationship.

Most people can navigate the first three phases, but that's not the primary goal of this book. It's the fourth phase that will lead you to the bliss you've always dreamed of, reminiscent of those fairy tales about princesses and Cinderella.

Phase 1:

The Crush Phase

This typically emerges generally after a few dates. If you don't feel a spark or develop a crush on the person you're dating by then, it's likely time to move on. This initial attraction, often referred to as infatuation, carries a slightly negative connotation, as it can imply that the relationship is driven solely by fleeting physical desire. While this may be true, experiencing infatuation is often a necessary step on the path to the deeper love you ultimately seek. Infatuation can indeed evolve into love, but the confusion between the two can lead many relationships to falter. This book will delve deeply into defining what love really is so you do not end up confusing it with infatuation.

Phase 2:

The Research Phase

This begins when you recognize enough positive qualities in someone to consider yourselves "dating." This is the time for intimate exploration, as you delve into what makes each other tick. What are their likes and dislikes? How do you connect on an emotional level? This stage is thrilling because everything feels new and full of potential. You're eager to learn as much as possible about each other. It's during this phase that you'll assess whether you're ready to commit to a long-term relationship.

Phase 3:

The Commitment Phase

This phase often culminates in marriage, but it can also encompass long-term committed relationships. At this stage, you're both willing to invest the effort necessary to build a future together. Many couples reach this point, but getting here doesn't guarantee anything. Instead of viewing this as the endgame—a common misconception—you should see it as the beginning to a deeper journey.

Think of it like an aspiring athlete aiming to enter a professional sports league, such as the National Basketball Association (NBA). Signing an NBA contract may feel like the pinnacle of success, but it's only the starting line. Now they must perform at a high level week after week to avoid being cut from the team while pursuing a championship. The same applies to marriage; it signifies your entry into the league of a legal commitment, but it doesn't ensure long-term success or happiness. It merely gives you a shot at achieving the ultimate goal: a loving and fulfilling relationship with the same person for a lifetime.

If you want the best chance of experiencing the relationship of your dreams—the kind you see in movies and read about in romantic novels—you'll need to embrace and learn to live through the final phase.

Phase 4:
Never Leaving

This phase represents the pinnacle of your relationship—the most fulfilling and pleasurable stage. Here, your significant other becomes the central focus of your life, and you live with the clarity that nothing can stand in the way of your bond. Every decision you make reflects consideration for their feelings and well-being. This deep connection typically develops after many years of marriage.

While the Commitment Phase and the Never Leaving Phase may seem similar, a significant distinction exists between them. People can be committed to various aspects of life—until they're not. Your commitment can wane or even disappear entirely. Consider how often you've felt dedicated to something, only to lose that commitment later. Beyond romantic relationships, think of times you may have drifted away from commitments to fitness, healthy eating, a favorite sports team, or even a political party.

In contrast, Never Leaving represents the highest level of commitment, where nothing can deter you from being together. You'll stand by each other through thick and thin, persevering through good times and bad. You'll be willing to do whatever it takes to keep your relationship as your number one priority.

This is the ultimate goal of this book: to guide you toward a state of the ultimate bliss. It's the moment you realize both of you are wholeheartedly committed to nurturing a happy, passionate relationship—when you reach the point of *Never Leaving.*

Phase 1

THE
CRUSH

To Catch
the Right Fish,
You Need
the Right Bait

In my twenties, I lifted weights regularly and had a pretty decent set of triceps and biceps. I also made sure I did a good job of making sure other people know about it. Whenever I went out with friends, I'd throw on a tight black T-shirt and jeans to show off my "guns." I certainly wasn't a hot looking guy, but I did attract a fair share of attention from women at social gatherings, many of whom I ended up dating. However, I found myself on this hamster wheel of continuously dating women that were not good for me. Were these women drawn to me for my mind or just my muscles? Did I put out the right bait to catch the right fish?

If you dress in a way that highlights specific body parts, you'll naturally attract people drawn to those traits. If you have big muscles and you dress in a way so that people can see them, the people that will most likely pursue you will be the people that like large muscles. The same goes for other body parts: breasts, legs, or whatever parts you have that stand out and can bring you attention. The attention you attract will likely shape your social circle, often leading to relationships based on these physical traits. Then those are the people that you will end up dating more often than not. Ask yourself: do you want a relationship built on physical appeal or something deeper? Which foundation is more likely to foster a lasting connection?

This is a crucial question you need to ask yourself when you are going on a date, a singles event, or just out trying to meet new people. Consider this scenario:

A young woman is preparing for an interview at a prestigious investment banking firm. She invites her best friend over for a fashion consultation. Her friend suggests a slinky dress with a revealing blouse, but the young woman firmly insists that she wants to be hired for her skills and qualifications, not her body. The friend then questions why she chooses to wear that same outfit when going out to bars and clubs trying to meet men.

What this story is conveying is that the way you dress determines who you will attract. She wants to be taken seriously when getting a job, but a job is often short lived. But when going out to try to meet a man that you hope leads to a life long commitment, it's okay not to be taken seriously? What kind of bait is she putting out to fish in the waters of the dating pool?

Back to my weightlifting, not only did I *not* meet the love of my life, I was stuck in this constant loop of meeting people who didn't connect to me on an emotional or intellectual level. I did not have the right bait on my fishing line. I certainly was reeling in plenty of fish, but unfortunately, they were not my favorite kind of fish. I was catching gefilte fish when I really wanted seared halibut. I certainly didn't want someone who was merely attracted to my muscles. It was only when I matured, that I realized that if I wanted to find the right person to marry, I needed to shift my focus from my body, to my soul.

Having an impressive physique might increase your chances of attracting attention, but will that attention lead to a meaningful relationship? Those who are drawn to you solely for your looks are often more likely to become part of the divorce statistics. So, what kind of bait should you use to attract someone to the real you?

To let your personality shine and enhance your chances of a fantastic relationship, consider dressing modestly. This means that you dress in a way that doesn't call unnecessary attention to the physical parts of you. It allows all the other parts of you to shine.

You can be attractive without being attracting. When you dress modestly, your intellectual and emotional self will be the focus, not your body. It doesn't mean that you have to don an armored suit or hijab; it just means that you are reserving the best parts of you for that special person. You will position yourself for a more meaningful connection—one that will lead you to the phase of "Never Leaving."

"You can be attractive without being attracting"

Clarify
Why You are Dating

In a small town, a woman was preparing to marry at the age of ninety. A local newspaper reporter visited her home to cover the story. When he asked about her future husband, she revealed that he was the town's funeral director. She then shared that she had been married three times before: first to a Wall Street investment banker in her twenties, then to a Broadway show producer in her thirties, and later to a priest in her late seventies. Now, at ninety, she was set to marry a funeral director. Curiously, the reporter asked why she had chosen such a diverse array of men as husbands. With a twinkle in her eye, she replied, "I married one for the money, two for the show, three to get ready, and four to go."

This whimsical story highlights a crucial point: when seeking love, you must clarify why you are dating. Are you merely seeking physical pleasure? If that's the case, dating is easy since your only requirement will be finding someone who can satisfy that desire. However, be cautious—entering into a physical relationship for fun can quickly escalate, leading to confusion between infatuation and love. This ambiguity can make it difficult to make sound decisions about the relationship. While it is possible for casual dating to lead to a successful relationship, it is just that the odds are way out of your favor to get to the phase of "Never Leaving."

Once your emotions take over, your intellect goes straight out the window. Engaging in physical intimacy clouds your judgment and heightens emotions, increasing the likelihood of regrettable decisions.

If you are dating for the purpose of getting married, you are pretty certain of what you are looking for. Ask yourself, "Is your date truly marriage material?" Dating becomes serious when you are dating with marriage in mind. You should have a pretty solid conviction of the qualities you're seeking and the values that matter to you. Unfortunately, without a clear vision of what you want, you're more likely to settle and compromise on your values.

I've encountered numerous couples who date for years without the willingness to commit to marriage. Wouldn't you think that dating for more than a few months should be enough time to see if you are compatible? What are people waiting for? Why would anyone remain in a relationship indefinitely without a commitment? Often, people linger in relationships due to physicality or a lack of clarity regarding their dating goals. This approach can create a false sense of comfort, which is not conducive to building a passionate marriage.

While it may not be practical, an ideal way to date or evaluate a potential partner would be to "interview" them behind a curtain, completely removing the physical aspect from the equation. By doing this, your decision would be based entirely on emotional connection and meaningful conversation, rather than being influenced by their appearance. This approach would allow you to focus on the deeper compatibility that truly sustains long-term relationships.

In certain religious communities, potential dates are often thoroughly vetted in advance, typically by the parents. Before their child even meets their date, the parents have already researched the family background, lifestyle, religious beliefs, and overall compatibility between the two individuals. They check references and ensure that both sides are aligned on core values and life goals. Only after both families approve does the couple go on a date. This takes a lot of work, but isn't it worth it? This is the biggest decision that anyone makes in their life! How you choose is the difference between Never Leaving and just being another failed marriage statistic.

Another strategy to evaluate compatibility is to consult a dating coach or someone who can play that role. This person can help you identify both the merits and potential pitfalls of a budding relationship. Ideally, your coach should know you well and be willing to offer honest feedback rather than simply telling you what you want to hear. You don't need a "yes" person—what you require is someone who will challenge you with the truth, even if it's difficult to accept. This individual might be a colleague, a relative, or even a trusted parent. The primary goal of a dating coach is to help you avoid significant mistakes in your search for a meaningful relationship.

You may have already fallen in love with someone who isn't the right fit for you, which is why trusting your dating coach's opinion is crucial. It's equally important to be willing to truly listen to their advice, especially because love can blind us to red flags. Your coach, unlike you, isn't emotionally invested in the relationship. Their perspective is grounded in logic and objectivity, with only your best interests at heart. This detachment allows them to see the relationship clearly and provide guidance that you may overlook.

Case Study: A former student of mine once called me from overseas, seeking advice about a guy she was dating. She admired that he was a go-getter and nearly finished with dental school. But then came the dreaded 'but.'

She explained that he was so busy with his studies that he barely had time to talk to her. She made excuses for him, blaming his hectic schedule and upcoming finals. Then she mentioned that he sometimes drove recklessly, scaring her, and occasionally cursed at other drivers. Although she told him she didn't appreciate this behavior, he continued doing it. Again, she excused it, saying he was under a lot of stress.

When I asked how many dates they'd been on, she said five. I pointed out that if she was already making so many excuses for him while they were dating—when most people are on their best behavior—what might that say about his behavior in a long-term marriage?

She struggled to see these as red flags because she was so focused on his positive qualities. She kept justifying his actions, trying to keep the relationship alive. After our conversation gave her some clarity, she decided to end the relationship, recognizing it wasn't the healthy foundation she deserved.

It's often said that love is blind. Love is not blind. Infatuation will make you blind! If a person is infatuated, they may not see any flaws in the person they are dating, but the guidance of a wise friend or coach can provide clarity. Think of it like renovating your kitchen: when you ask a friend for their opinion, are you really asking for their perspective? Probably not. You're seeking validation rather than genuine feedback. You want them to say, "I love it!" If you really wanted their opinion, you would have asked them *before* the renovation. When you ask for someone's opinion on the person you are dating, don't look for validation, seek the truth.

What are the odds that you will meet the love of your life randomly in a bar? It does happen, but those odds are low. In a typical scenario, you meet someone either through a social event, a dating app, or maybe on a blind date and then engage in one of the first 2 phases of love.

After a month or two of the Research Phase, you begin to figure out if it is still worth investing in the relationship or not. However, if physical intimacy enters the picture, it can complicate the relationship making it harder to walk away, often out of fear of loneliness. Some may even seek new partners while still involved with someone else, jumping ship as soon as they find a replacement. While this approach can lead to a new relationship, achieving the "Never Leaving" milestone requires a more deliberate effort.

If you begin the dating process with clarity on what your purpose for dating is, you will less likely be caught in a relationship that deep down you don't really want to be in. If you really want to get married, be clear about it and tell yourself that you will not continue with any exclusive dating unless you feel that the person you are dating has the potential for marriage.

Date Them,
Don't Mate Them

Once you bring physicality into a relationship, you lower the chance of getting to the phase of Never Leaving. Why is this? Because once someone makes that physical connection, intellect goes out the window and then you may confuse infatuation with love.

I realize that many young people dating may disagree with this chapter, but this book isn't just about finding a spouse—it's about finding a partner for a passionate, lifelong relationship.

Just because you share physical intimacy with someone doesn't mean they're suited to be a lifelong partner. Don't confuse a physical relationship with true compatibility for marriage. Perception is crucial in dating—when you present yourself as casual or uncommitted, others may see you that way too, making them less likely to invest in a lasting relationship.

We can learn an important lesson about perception from Sidney Frank, a successful businessman who rose to prominence in the wine and spirits industry. His initial success stemmed from the popularity of Jägermeister, a liquor known for its distinct black licorice flavor—at least, that's what I was told.

In 1977, he launched Grey Goose vodka to compete with other super-premium liquors. To convey a sense of exclusivity, he had it produced in France, knowing that consumers often associate higher prices with French products—though that logic doesn't seem to apply to French cars or French fries.

Frank marketed Grey Goose as the best-tasting vodka in the world, pricing it similarly to Absolut Vodka, another top-tier brand. However, Frank wasn't satisfied with the sales of his new liquor.

Interestingly, according to the American Food and Drug Administration, vodka is a grain-neutral spirit. Although many may disagree with this statement, probably because they don't want to have been considered duped their entire adult life, it is impossible to tell the difference between any brand of non-flavored vodka if it is filtered more than 3 times. This is even more so when it's in a cosmopolitan or any other mixed drink. This means that there was only way someone could differentiate from what they thought was the quality of a vodka; and that was by price.

So Sidney Frank pulled out a strategy that lives in the Hall of Fame of marketing. He doubled the price of his vodka. Grey Goose was now the most expensive vodka on the market, eclipsing Absolut by a wide margin. His theory was based that consumers just assumed that the higher priced vodka was better. His marketing strategy worked and his brand became so popular that Sidney Frank sold the Grey Goose brand to Bacardi in 2004 for a staggering $2.3 billion. In the end, there was only one thing that actually distinguished one brand from another—and that was perception.

People tend to assign value based on two key criteria: price and accessibility. If something is priced low, it's perceived to be of lesser value; conversely, if it's expensive, it's generally considered to be of higher quality. This is why companies invest heavily in marketing and advertising—to create a perceived value around their products.

Consider the fashion industry: is a handbag really worth tens of thousands of dollars? Perhaps if you're a real estate agent in Beverly Hills. Fashion designers have skillfully convinced consumers that carrying a Louis Vuitton, Fendi, or Lana Marks purse will enhance their self-esteem. In reality, that's merely a short-term placebo for deeper insecurities. If owning a Chanel purse could cure depression, psychologists would be out of business!

If something is hard to get, or more exclusive, then the perception is that it is more valuable. People will wait as long as they need to get something they perceive as exclusive. When something is inaccessible, it becomes more desirable. There is a famous line in dating, "people want what they can't have." There is some truth to this.

For example, when the musical Hamilton premiered, tickets sold out in a flash, making it one of Broadway's hottest shows. The demand for tickets exceeded rationality, with shows booked months to a year in advance and prices soaring to over $1,000 each, far exceeding their original cost.

The same phenomenon occurs with new toys during the holiday shopping season. When a hot toy hits the market, the excitement becomes self-reinforcing; everyone suddenly "has to have it." People even camp outside stores like Walmart overnight just to be the first in line for that coveted item. If consumers knew that a store would receive a shipment of tens of thousands of the toy, many might not bother waiting in line at all. It's precisely the lack of availability that enhances desirability.

When it comes to dating, you are essentially marketing yourself. Why would you want to cheapen your brand? People often perceive items with a lower price tag or greater accessibility as less valuable. Do you want to be valued as a rare and precious individual? Dress like royalty, and you will be treated as such.

If you make certain aspects of yourself readily available to everyone, you risk being perceived similarly to low-end brands like Smirnoff vodka or Boone's Farm wine. You might be seen as a "human doing" rather than a "human being," reducing your worth to what you can offer physically. If that's your intention in dating, you're probably not the target audience for this book.

How we present ourselves is critical; people form judgments based on appearance. The more accessible you make yourself physically, the more likely you are to be valued for your body rather than your mind and soul. To put it bluntly, why would someone commit to purchasing the merchandise if they can get it for free?

This book is not about finding someone to date. There are plenty of books about that subject. This book is about finding someone who can be your passionate, loving partner for the rest of your life. Someone who is Never Leaving.

As we discussed earlier, clarifying your dating intentions is essential. If you're dating without the goal of marriage, then you can afford to share parts of yourself freely. But if you're seeking a lifelong commitment, think carefully before you give away your value. If you believe that not sleeping with your date will drive them away, consider that they may not have been genuinely interested in you to begin with—they might have just been drawn to how you made them feel. If they truly valued you for who you are, they would be willing to wait.

Imagine this scenario: after two dates, you decide to sleep with someone. The next morning, you wake up to find your date rifling through your checkbook. Would you be upset? If so, if someone knowing your financial matters upsets you more than someone knowing your body, you may need to think about your priorities in life.

If you date them to mate them, it may end up that you now hate them. This is not the way to get to Never Leaving.

You must present yourself as the most valuable entity in the world. Don't price yourself just like the low-end vodkas because you are diminishing your worth. You are every bit as valuable as the most valuable brands in the world, because you are the Grey Goose!

The Three Date Rule

The Three Date Rule means that you should date someone at least three times unless there are obvious signs that they are one and done, such as:

- They live in a treehouse

- They talk incessantly about their mother

- They laugh like a hyena

Okay, maybe those aren't *all* of the reasons you should not date someone again, but it's a good start.

Why the Three Date Rule? Dating can be awkward, and it's often challenging to truly get to know someone on the first date. If there are no glaring red flags, it's wise to give it another shot. Three dates provide a reasonable timeframe to move past initial nervousness and form a deeper connection. Knowing you'll give a potential partner at least three chances can alleviate the pressure of the first date.

There's also a phenomenon called "First Date Bias," which suggests that the more attractive someone is, the higher the likelihood of a second date.

"First Date Bias:
The better looking they are,
the higher the probability of a second date"

As a man, I can admit that many of us feel incredibly nervous when dating. While I can't speak for women, I've heard that they often share similar feelings. The prospect of dating can evoke fear—sometimes even more than a visit to the dentist! Why? Because many men can feel intimidated by very attractive women.

When I was dating, I was so nervous that it affected what I would order at a restaurant. Spilling food on myself was always a possibility and wearing a bib would probably not help me get me a second date. So forget about pasta–invariably the sauce would end up on my shirt. I would always play it as safe as possible and only order a salad with plain lettuce, no dressing. That's because carrots can give you gas, avocado may smear all over your sleeve, and the tomatoes can get stuck in your teeth. So if this is the way I acted on my first date, doesn't it seem obvious that you really won't get to know me on one date?

You might not immediately fall in love on the first date, but you are influenced by their appearance whether you realize it or not. Because of our natural bias towards appearance, the more physically attracted we are on the date, the more likely that we will pursue the relationship. Since it's difficult to connect emotionally on the first date, we rely on what we see. In order to connect with someone emotionally and intellectually, you should date someone at least three times so you have a chance to get to know them.

Scientific evidence supports this notion. In Malcolm Gladwell's best-selling book Blink, he discusses how, prior to the

1980s, orchestras predominantly hired male musicians. This led to a widespread belief that men were inherently better musicians. However, once screens were introduced during auditions, allowing judges to hear rather than see the musicians, more women began to be hired. This high-lighted how decision-makers were influenced by visual biases—something that also rings true in dating.

In fact, if we wanted the best chance of finding a suitable partner, we might consider meeting for the first time behind a screen. This setup would eliminate physical bias, allowing us to focus on emotional and intellectual connections. Imagine spending an evening together without seeing one another—by the end, you would know if there's a genuine connection, without the bias of physical appearances.

You may have experienced a similar experience at a friend's wedding, meeting their future spouse for the first time and doing a double-take at their appearance. You might wonder how your attractive friend ended up with someone who looks like Freddy Krueger or Ms. Piggy. The reason they are marrying them is you don't know them like your friend does. The stronger the emotional and intellectual connection, the more attractive that person becomes to you. This underscores the importance of sticking to the Three Date Rule—don't miss out on an incredible person just because of initial perceptions.

The more you get to know someone you like, the better looking they become! Conversely, the more you learn about someone you dislike, the less attractive they are to you.

For every gorgeous person out there, there's someone who is sick of them. So, if you find someone marginally attractive on the first date, remember that giving them a bit more time could reveal an amazing personality underneath.

A vibrant personality can enhance attractiveness significantly, and you may miss out on a fantastic partner due to your first date bias.

Following the Three Date Rule will help you to get over this First Date Bias...unless they laugh like a hyena.

"For every gorgeous woman
or handsome guy walking down the street,
there is probably someone
who is sick of them"

Beware of the
New Face Factor

There's an issue I encountered during my single days that can lead some people, especially men, to make poor dating decisions: The New Face Factor. Picture this: you're out at a bar with friends and spot a large table of single women. As a single male, it's hard not to notice a group of attractive women, especially when they are all dressed to the nines. This initial excitement can lead someone to date a person they might not have considered in a different setting. Why is this problematic? In the moment, it's easy to feel overwhelmed by the sheer number of women you may initially find appealing. With hair styled in voluminous waves, enough jewelry to rival a Tiffany's showroom, and perfume so overwhelming that even Pepé Le Pew would retreat, this sensory overload often clouds your judgment. While they may all look stunning, it's important to remember that each person at that table may have flaws. Assessing individual personalities becomes nearly impossible with such a large group.

The energy of the moment, with everyone seemingly having a great time, can easily lead to a misleading first impression. This is like a child walking into a toy store, dazzled by everything at once. It's only when you take the time to see each person individually that you can truly understand who they are.

The surprising thing is, the person you may end up dating—or even marrying—could be the one you barely notice at first. In the midst of a large group, with so many distractions, it's easy to overlook her. That's why the "new face" effect plays a big role, and it's one reason why three dates are crucial. By the third date, her face is no longer new, allowing you to see beyond initial impressions and you can truly get to know her.

When dating, we can easily be blinded by various factors, leading us to overlook significant flaws. The more desperate we are to find a partner, the more likely we are to dismiss red flags in favor of surface-level attraction. We may find ourselves drawn to the best-dressed, most outgoing, or flashiest person in the room—but this can be a significant misstep.

Be mindful not to let the novelty of a new face keep you dating someone even after you've realized they have qualities you genuinely dislike. It's easy to be swept up by initial attraction, but lasting relationships require more than surface-level appeal. Trust your instincts when red flags emerge, rather than ignoring them just because the excitement is still fresh.

Generally, men and women perceive each other differently: men tend to assess women from the outside in, while women often evaluate men from the inside out. While women appreciate a good-looking man, intelligence is typically a non-negotiable trait. Conversely, men may overlook a lack of intelligence in a beautiful woman, continuing to pursue her for her looks. It's only about after the 3rd date that the lack of intelligence will override any level of beauty.

Imagine you're at a singles event with your bestie, and you spot a gorgeous guy across the room. Excited, you point him out, and she tells you he's one of her coworkers. When she asks if you want to meet him, you eagerly agree. Together, you weave through the crowd to meet this 6'4" Fabio lookalike.

At first glance, he seems perfect—until he starts talking. Within 30 seconds, you realize he has all the looks, but has probably never read any books. He has the body of an athlete, but the intellect of a bird. He's all looks and no substance. Would you date him? Not a chance!

Now, imagine you're at a singles event with your best buddy. You spot a stunning woman across the bar—the most beautiful woman you've ever seen. Your friend knows her and offers to introduce you. Excited, you follow him over, and she's even more breathtaking up close. Then she starts talking, and you quickly realize that God must have ran out of personality when she was born. Are you still going to pursue her? As a man, your first instinct might be to rationalize: She's so gorgeous—maybe she's just pretending to be boring to keep guys from constantly hitting on her. You convince yourself that once you start dating, her true self will shine through.

After the first date, you enjoy the attention and envious stares when you walk into the restaurant with her, but you realize the meal would have been more satisfying alone. By the second date, you're starting to wonder if you're the one lacking intelligence for sticking it out. By the third date, you can't stand her anymore and feel a mix of relief and pity—relief for yourself and pity for the poor guy who ends up with her.

To avoid falling prey to the New Face Factor, approach dating with a clean slate and without preconceived notions.

When you meet someone without any prior knowledge about them, you set yourself up to judge them without bias. Consider how your perceptions could shift if you knew a date came from a wealthy family or was known to be genuinely kind. Such insights could undoubtedly influence your interest and the outcome of your date. However, if you hear that your date has commitment issues, remember that they may simply not have found the right person yet. That person could be you!

Have you ever read a book and then later watched the movie? In my experience, and from what I've heard from others, the movie is almost never as good as the book. But why is that? It's because it's never as exciting when you already know the ending. The same logic applies when you've read a review of the movie beforehand—it takes away the element of surprise and the sense of discovery, making the experience feel less thrilling.

I once watched "Swept Away," starring Madonna and Guy Ritchie, during a flight. I had never heard of it and genuinely enjoyed the film. Later, I discovered it was deemed one of the worst movies of the year, grossing only one million dollars worldwide—less than what Goobers sells in theaters! Had I read the reviews first, I probably wouldn't have watched it at all.

Not having any preconceived notions is crucial in dating. This is why you should date someone thinking they are a clean slate! Imagine your date as an empty white board with nothing on it. Evaluating the *potential* of your date can be more important than how they are at the moment. Remember that geeky guy in High School that no one dated? He is now gorgeous, successful entrepreneur, plus he has a heart of gold. You probably didn't notice that potential when you knew him.

One last idea I want to share with you is about your face. Your face is a new face to anyone you meet for the first time. How you present your face determines a lot about how others look at you! How often do you see your own face? Definitely not nearly as much as others sees it. Your facial expressions are a reflection of you. If everyone else sees your face much more than you do, that means that you better make sure that it looks happy! Have you ever seen the picture of someone with a pouty face versus a picture of them with a smile? It makes a huge difference in their appearance! Not only is the New Face Factor something to consider for someone else, but you also need to consider that your face is also being scrutinized as a New Face Factor. How you look is how people perceive you, so put a smile on that face!

The Feeling of Being in Love

Before diving into a romantic relationship, it's essential to establish a common definition of what love means. This is crucial because your understanding of love may differ significantly from that of the person you're dating or married to. Defining your terms before getting serious can help you avoid many potential misunderstandings and headaches down the line. At the very least, you should reach a common understanding on what love means to both of you, even if it differs from this book.

Clarifying your definition of love is vital, as it is frequently confused with infatuation. While infatuation can evolve into genuine love, identifying when this transition occurs—or if it will happen at all—can be challenging and can lead to a relationship filled with disappointment. How many couples do you know have said after their divorce, "What I was thinking when I married this person?" Unfortunately, this is a common occurrence. The answer to this question is that they were *not* thinking because they were infatuated.

I'd like to expand on our understanding of love by explor-
ing not only its definition, but also what it feels like to
be in love. The definition and the feeling of love are two
separate components.

The feeling of being in love means wanting to give to someone without any expectation of receiving anything in return. In contrast, infatuation is often a fleeting moment
of desire driven by an attraction to something you want.
It's essentially a chemical reaction in the brain that can
cloud your judgment and hinder logical decision-making.

Many marriages happen because of infatuation rather than
true love. People are infatuated with those they are attracted to, but they love those they are infatuated with *and*
invest in. When we genuinely love someone, our instinct
is to want to give to them. This is evident in our relationships with our children; we provide for them without
expecting anything back—except grandchildren!

"The feeling of love is when you want to give to someone without expecting anything in return"

Rabbi Abraham Twerski, a well-known psychologist,
warns about a concept called "fish love."[2] "Fish love"
means you found someone who could provide you with
all of your physical and emotional needs. For example,
if you love to eat fish, it's because it tastes good, not because you love fish. We don't really love fish, because
if we did, we wouldn't fillet it and eat it for dinner. Instead,
we would put it on our nightstand in a bowl of water,
read it fish stories at night and take it to the park for fish
playdates! Now that's crazy because we don't love fish;

we love the pleasure and taste that the fish brings us. Fish love means each partner is looking out for themselves for what they can get out of the relationship. The other person becomes just a vehicle for their gratification.

On the other hand, real love is what you have when the relationship is not about getting, but about giving. Because when we give to someone, and I don't mean just baubles from Tiffany, we are investing ourselves in them. Giving of our heart, emotions, vulnerability, time, and attention is really investing a bit of ourselves. We are giving them an opening into our feelings, desires, and emotions. Because the ultimate gift you can give to someone is to be emotionally available for them.

Ultimately, since we love ourselves more than anyone else, if we give something of ourselves to someone else, we ultimately love them as well. This is why when relationships are just based on giving of gifts, they are probably compensating for the lack of emotional availability that they are providing to each other. There are many women driving their BMW to the country club given to them by their husbands who eventually became their ex-husbands.

This is why people who struggle to be emotionally available have a much harder time with relationships. This is what real love is based on. If we carry emotional scars from previous relationships, such as a heart-wrenching breakup, or the impact from living with dysfunctional families, we may find ourselves internally wounded, requiring time to heal before we are capable of a healthy relationship.

Since the feeling of love requires giving to others without wanting anytime in return, you must be willing to give of yourself which requires vulnerability. If you can't be willing to open your heart to someone else, then you'll have a hard time giving of yourself to others.

Defining Love

Having already explained what it feels like to be in love, it is now time to define what love truly is. Why offer both an emotional perspective and a definition? Because when you ask someone how they know they're in love, they often respond with what they are feeling, which is subjective. Feelings can be powerful, but can they ever lead us astray? I'll let you answer that.

The definition of love is the emotional pleasure you feel when you recognize another person's virtues and you continue to appreciate them throughout your life. To put it another way, everyone has idiosyncrasies, so you better stay focused on why you fell in love in the first place!

Almost anyone you decide to marry is eventually going to cause you some sort of pain—it's an inevitability of relationships. To reach the stage of "Never Leaving," you must continually remind yourself of the reasons you chose to marry that person.

This is why only having infatuation for someone will not last. That feeling will eventually go away. You need the infatuation to get you started, but you will need it to evolve into so much more. Unfortunately, many couples lose sight of the qualities that initially attracted them, allowing minor faults to overshadow their partner's virtues.

Consider your children, if you have any. Do they have flaws? Most likely. Yet, no one falls out of love with their children. Even parents of serial murderers may continue to love their children, despite their actions. You don't choose your children, but you are the one that chose your spouse! So why do parents maintain their love for their children, regardless of their behavior, while many are quick to divorce when a spouse's actions disappoint them?

People often get divorced because they lose sight on why they got married in the first place. There were reasons why you fell in love and you got married. What happened to those reasons? Over time, those reasons can fade into the background as you start to focus more on your spouse's flaws, rather than the bond that initially united you.

It's crucial to have a strategy that can help you stay focused on why you decided to get married in the first place. Let's draw a concept from the analogy from the popular cooking show "Chopped" on the Food Network.

Chopped:
Fire Up
Your Relationship!

The show begins with four contestants vying for the title of "Chopped Champion." They have just fifteen minutes to prepare an appetizer, which is then judged. After the first round, one contestant is eliminated, and the remaining three chefs face off in a second round with twenty minutes to create a main course. Following that, another chef is "chopped," leaving the final two contestants to craft a dessert for the championship. The twist? Before the competition starts, each chef opens a mystery basket filled with unusual ingredients that must be incorporated into their dishes. These items are often so peculiar that even experienced chefs may have never encountered them—think crocodile tail, snake meat, black squid ink, dried crickets or snail urine. Okay, I made that last one up.

The chefs scramble to devise a plan for using these ingredients in their recipes, much like the challenges faced in marriage. Each of us brings our own unique character traits to a relationship, some of which may be unfamiliar to our partner. These traits can range from seemingly minor issues, like laziness or impatience, to more significant concerns, such as trust issues, emotional disconnect, or inflated egos. Often, these deficiencies don't surface as serious problems until years into the marriage. A potential spouse might notice that their partner has a short temper, but may not deem it significant enough to end the relationship. Fast forward twenty years, and that anger might intensify—or it may simply become more noticeable now that you share a home.

In essence, we must learn to "make a dish" together with our partner. While we may be unaware of our own quirks, we also need to navigate each other's emotional complexities. Despite our best efforts over the years, some relationships can become strained when the challenges feel insurmountable.

Remember, everyone has issues—no one is perfect. However, there is someone who is perfect for you. Real love flourishes when you concentrate on your partner's virtues rather than their faults. By adopting this perspective, you equip yourself with the tools needed to embark on any relationship with a greater chance of success. If you're really want "fish love," go marry a salmon!

Square Peg
Into Round Hole

Many people in the dating scene often claim they are searching for the "right person"—someone who seamlessly fits with their personality and into their lifestyle. However, this mindset can inadvertently create barriers that limit your chances of finding a meaningful relationship. So, how can you increase your odds of finding that "perfect" match? By expanding your horizons and embracing a wider variety of lifestyles and personalities, especially if you've been dating for years without success.

Imagine a one-year-old playing with a shape sorter. The child diligently tries to fit the appropriately shaped pegs into their corresponding holes. If the child has a hard time with this, frustration may set in and they might remove the lid and start throwing the pegs in haphazardly. This mirrors the dating experience for many individuals. Searching for that one person who perfectly fits your criteria can be frustrating. To improve your chances of meeting the right partner, consider removing the barriers that you put up that keeps you from dating people you may not have initially considered.

I've encountered many men in their 40s and 50s who remain single despite being financially stable and relatively well-adjusted. When I ask them if they want to get married, they all say yes. Yet, I suspect some of them aren't being entirely honest with themselves. They may feel pressured by societal expectations to want marriage, fearing they'll seem odd or selfish if they don't. The real reason they stay single often has more to do with a struggle to open themselves to love, either by accepting love or giving it fully.

The same may be true for middle-aged men and women who insist they *don't* want to marry. Deep down, they may crave a loving relationship, but use this excuse to avoid facing their discomfort with vulnerability. The desire is there, but the fear of being open keeps it out of reach.

Another common issue arises when these same men present me with an exhaustive list of requirements for a potential spouse: dark skin, slender build, heights between 5'4" and 5'6", an exceptional cook, wealthy, and brilliantly funny. I can't help but wonder—how likely are they to find someone who meets such specific criteria? Do you think they will ever get married? The reality is that they're building walls that prevent them from opening their hearts and inviting someone special into their lives.

Case study: A 29-year-old single man visited me recently for dinner. Despite being handsome, funny, and exceptionally intelligent, he struggled to find a partner. When I suggested a few wonderful women around 25-27 years old, he shocked me by stating he only dates women aged 22 or 23. When I pressed for an explanation, he simply said he wasn't *attracted to women older than that. At that moment, I felt an urge to reach over the table and smack him in the face. I asked him, what would happen if he married a 22-year-old woman? In four years, would he not find her attractive? Of course, he had no good answer. His rigid standards were erecting an impenetrable wall between him and the possibility of finding a lifelong partner.*

Limiting your dating pool to a narrow set of criteria can severely restrict your chances of marriage. To foster more opportunities, you must be open to various "shapes and sizes" of potential partners. It's crucial to let go of the mental image of what your spouse should look like or their career path. This also involves being less critical of others' imperfections and acknowledging that you, too, have your own flaws. Everyone has them! Even if you believe you've found the "perfect" person, that doesn't mean they are perfect—just perfect for you.

This brings us to the next key idea, one that should become your dating mantra.

You Don't Know Your Type... Until You Meet Your Type

How many times have you tried setting someone up, only to hear, "They're not my type"? This often happens when the person barely knows anything about the potential match—sometimes from just a picture. In those moments, a perfect opportunity could be slipping away—wasted simply because of superficial judgments.

There was a single woman whom I crossed paths with on numerous occasions. I had decided that I wanted to make a strong effort to help her find a spouse. At nearly 40 years old, her beauty was undeniable. In addition to her good looks, she exuded intelligence and was very passionate. It was clear that she had the potential to make some man very happy. I saw what I thought was low hanging fruit. I had already had some success with matchmaking so it's possible I was a bit over confident.

The first person I had successfully matched was a man in his late 70s from Denver who was eager to be in a committed relationship. He was a dedicated student of mine, absorbing all the wisdom I shared in my dating and marriage classes. After attending a number of sessions, he asked if he could treat me to lunch, which I gladly accepted. After getting to know him better, I offered to post his picture on my Facebook page to help him find a partner. To my delight, I connected him with a retired woman who had recently moved to Costa Rica.

It wasn't one of the 1800 "friends" I had on Facebook that would end up becoming his girlfriend. Instead, it was through the friends of friends, the vast network that I had access to. If each of my "friends" knew just three single older women, that would have been almost 5000 potential dates he would not have otherwise met. Finding a spouse doesn't need to be like finding a needle in a haystack. You just have to make the haystack smaller or increase the number of needles. In this case, I successfully increased the number of potential needles in his haystack.

"Finding a spouse doesn't need to be like finding a needle in a haystack. You just have to make the haystack smaller or increase the number of needles"

My wife and I played a pivotal role in bringing together another young couple. We had known both individuals from various circles in our lives, and we had a strong feeling that they were meant for each other. Our intuition proved to be correct, as they hit it off and ended up getting married.

Another couple that got married did so with my indirect assistance. I didn't directly set them up, but both parties acknowledge that without my help, they may never have crossed paths. The woman was setting up a booth in the Old City of Jerusalem to promote podcasts, but she had poor signage. I offered to help design a sign that would draw more attention. As fate would have it, the man who had initially turned her down for a date without meeting her noticed the newly improved sign. This encounter led to their relationship, and they are now happily married with a child. This was another instance of not knowing your type until you meet your type.

After successfully helping several couples find love, I decided to help this woman. I was assuming it would be as easy as my previous attempt on Facebook. However, what unfolded next is the reason you are reading about this story.

I received a message from a man in his late 40s expressing interest in the woman I posted about on Facebook. Impressed by our initial conversation, I decided to screen him first myself. Even though she had turned down several other men I found for her, I was confident she would not turn down someone that I personally investigated and endorsed.

I was very impressed by this man just from one meeting. Besides being very engaging and a pleasure to have coffee with, he had a masters in education. The most important aspect was that he had a job that he really loved. Now, from my perspective, the guy had a lot going for him. He checked off all the boxes I thought were important.

So I had decided to tell this woman about my find. I had a growing suspicion that the more information I provided, the less likely a date would materialize, so I did not show her a picture of him.

After presenting the idea of going out with this guy, she uttered four words that struck me like a hammer; "He's not my type." I couldn't help but wonder, "Seriously?" She hadn't even met or seen a picture of him. How could she dismiss him so readily? Especially when I was going out of my way to set her up!

This incident prompted me to ponder the nature of dating. How many people who eventually marry actually end up with someone who fits their initial "type"? I'm not aware of any research on this topic. Personally, I don't think my wife ever envisioned marrying a completely non-religious Jew, standing only 5 feet 8 inches tall, red hair, and working in the rare coin trade, a business no one has ever heard of.

Based on my personal experience, neither my wife nor I were each other's "type" initially. We only became each other's "type" after we met and got to know one another. I believe the secret to almost anyone finding their soulmate is that they have no idea what their type is until they meet them.

How do you have any clue what your type is? What you may have is a figment from your imagination of what you *think* you are looking for. It's likely fabricated from your past, perhaps from a childhood crush on someone with a particularly cute smile or certain color hair. That fleeting moment of attraction has shaped your perception of your "type" for years to come.

In the 1970s, Farrah Fawcett was a star on the TV show "Charlie's Angels." Her beauty captivated everyone, including my junior high school peers, who couldn't help but have crushes on her. I distinctly recall a classmate holding up a magazine with her picture on the front and giving the picture a big kiss. It was a bit surprising to see just how many boys had a crush on her.

As these teenagers grow up and begin contemplating marriage, many of them still hold onto the image of the ideal spouse they had in their youth: a blonde beauty resembling Farrah Fawcett. Some may even end up marrying a woman who fits this physical description. However, the issue arises when you realize that attraction based solely on appearance is fleeting. After a few years of marriage, you come to understand that there is so much more to a successful marriage than just physical beauty. What truly sustains a relationship is a deep connection on a soul level.

How can you truly know if someone is your "type" just from a picture? The truth is, you can't. From my dating experiences, there have been many instances where I saw a woman's picture before the date, only to find out that it either exaggerated her beauty or, more surprisingly, failed to do her justice.

So if you want to improve your chances of finding your soulmate, realize that you don't know your type, until you meet your type. Now let's try to gain clarity what kind of person will be good for you in a relationship.

The Soulmate Discovery Worksheet

Gain clarity on what you truly seek in a spouse! Get a blank piece of paper and spend just 30 minutes filling out this worksheet. You'll uncover new characteristics to look for in a partner that you may not have previously considered.

A. If you could live with any animal in the world, what would it be? List your 3 favorite qualities of your animal.

B. Brainstorm and list at least 5 qualities you desire in a spouse.

C. Think of happily married couples that you admire & list 3 qualities about them that make them special.

D. Identify a positive role model in your life (grandparent, friend, teacher, or public figure) and list 3 qualities you admire about them.

E. Identify and list 3 or more of your challenging traits.

Now, let's create a master list of the qualities that will contribute to your awesome marriage.

Copy the qualities from lists A, B, C, and D.

From List E, identify qualities that could balance out your challenging traits.

Now prioritize your new master list from 1 to 10.

If you find someone who possesses most of the top 10 qualities, especially the top 3, marry them!

By completing this worksheet, you've likely identified new characteristics to consider when dating. You've refined your search criteria and increased your chances of finding a compatible partner.

Next, we'll move on to the Research Phase, where you'll continue to learn essential tools to help decide whether or not to marry someone. Remember, you can choose to be happily married to a flawed individual or unhappily married to one. It's your choice to be happy.

Phase 2

THE
RESEARCH

This is what I consider the most exhilarating stage of any relationship! You've made it through the first few dates, and hopefully, you're still feeling that exciting rush of attraction that started in the Crush Phase. The initial awkwardness and "First Date Bias" are behind you, and the tension of the early encounters has melted away. Now comes the moment where you decide whether to take the relationship to the next level.

At this point, the phases of love begin to overlap. You may still be riding the wave of the initial crush, but simultaneously, you're starting to gather more insight into who this person truly is. It's the perfect blend of excitement and curiosity, where everything feels fresh, but you're also getting serious about where things might go.

The best part? It's likely still early enough that any deep-seated issues or "skeletons in the closet" haven't emerged. Don't worry—they'll surface in due time! For now, enjoy this stage where the possibilities seem endless and the excitement is palpable.

Learning to Listen

In my early 20s, I had lots of first dates, but struggled to get second dates. Then a friend gave me some invaluable advice: "Stop talking and just listen." He couldn't have been more right. I hadn't realized just how much I was dominating the conversation until I finally stopped talking and listened instead.

The strength of any relationship is rooted in how well you listen. When people talk about if they are dating, they often say, "I'm seeing someone." But the truth is, they should be saying, "I'm listening to someone."

After all, once you've seen a person, what's left to see again? A different colored suit or dress? Physical appearances are fleeting and become familiar quickly. But listening—truly listening—opens the door to endless discovery. You can see someone once and know what they look like, but you can listen to someone for a lifetime and still learn something new every time. Listening is what makes you part of the relationship.

It's remarkable that there are classes for public speaking everywhere, yet you rarely, if ever, hear of classes teaching public listening. If any exist, they're certainly not widespread. Marriage books often emphasize communication as the key to a successful relationship. But if you aren't genuinely listening to your partner, no amount of speaking will improve the communication.

True listening means deeply absorbing what someone is sharing, understanding it to the point where you can reflect it back with clarity and empathy. It's about being fully present and engaged, and that's what transforms a simple conversation into a meaningful relationship.

Listening is the key to capturing someone's heart. Interestingly, the word "heart" has "ear" right in the middle of it. When someone listens to you with their ears, they are, in a sense, holding you at the center of their heart.

When you truly listen to your partner, you're making them the focal point of your world. It's not just about hearing their words, but about fully engaging with what they're sharing. Think about the times you've been in an argument—while the other person was talking, were you probably crafting your response in your mind. In moments like that, you're hearing, but not really listening. Hearing is passive, it goes in one ear and out the other. Listening, however, is active—it's about focusing, processing, and deeply understanding what the other person is trying to convey.

An interesting observation: the word "listen" contains the same letters as "silent." To truly listen, you must quiet your mind, stop formulating responses, and be fully present. It requires your complete attention, undivided and patient.

For men especially, this can be a challenge. Men are natural problem-solvers, and often when their wives share something, they instinctively want to fix it. But sometimes, women don't want a solution—they just want someone to listen to them. Men must learn to listen to their partners without interrupting or immediately offering advice. This principle applies to any relationship, but it's especially important with your spouse. And dating is the perfect time to start practicing this essential skill.

Listening doesn't always come naturally, but like anything, the more you practice, the better you'll get. And the better you become at truly listening, the deeper and more meaningful your relationships will grow.

Sometimes one person is just looking for validation that their feelings are correct and that it is okay to feel the way they do. Validation means you understand the way they feel and you accept them for that, even if your reality is different from theirs. More important than trying to fix things for someone, is to just be there and to listen and validate that their feelings are okay. When a women's feelings are validated, *they* feel validated.

"When a women's feelings are validated, they feel validated."

Listening isn't just about hearing words—it's about fully processing and understanding what's being said. A great indicator of successful listening is your ability to accurately repeat what was said. The best courtroom attorneys excel because they can first articulate their opponent's argument, showing the judge or jury that they understand both sides before presenting their own case. Similarly, if you restate your spouse's or partner's perspective in any discussion or disagreement, it demonstrates a genuine effort to understand their point of view.

Clarifying their position aloud not only confirms that you've listened, but it also ensures that you're fully grasping their perspective. To truly connect, you must step into your partner's shoes and see things from their vantage point—understanding why they hold their opinions, even if you don't agree.

There will inevitably be times when your spouse or partner may not seem to listen. This doesn't mean they won't ever hear you; it just might require someone else to relay the message in a way that resonates. People often need to hear advice or opinions from a different source—perhaps a friend or a colleague—to absorb it fully.

Take a simple example: you might suggest trying a new restaurant that you've heard great things about, but your partner isn't interested. Later, if they hear the same recommendation from a friend, they might suddenly be more eager to go. Why? Because hearing it from someone else can give the suggestion more weight. Sometimes, we are so close to someone that they may not immediately recognize the value in what we're saying.

Finally, when communicating with someone, it's important to be direct and to the point. This applies not just to intimate relationships, but to all conversations. People have limited attention spans, and if you meander, the essence of what you want to convey can be lost. Get straight to the point, and your message will have a greater impact.

This also includes writing emails—often a single, well--crafted sentence is all it takes to convey your message. Clear, concise communication helps ensure your partner understands you fully, leaving less room for misunderstandings

Whenever I get home from my work, my wife needs to talk to me about her day, while I just want to grab a drink and relax. I have very little interest in talking, but I will sit and listen to her anyway because I know it's how she connects with me.

When it comes to dating, men should often take a step back and let the woman guide the conversation. If a man dominates the discussion, he can come off as arrogant or insecure. On the other hand, if he listens more, he'll likely be seen as a good listener, and she'll enjoy their time together. Of course, there are exceptions—if a woman is particularly quiet, a man who can lead the conversation will be appreciated. But generally speaking, allowing the woman to talk more is a winning approach.

Here are five tips for helping your partner (or anyone) truly listen to you:

- If you want other people to listen to *you,* they have to know that you listen to *them.* No one cares how much you know unless they know how much you care.

- No one will listen to you if you are a hypocrite. Your words must be backed up by action.

- Your words should be sincere and come from your heart. Words that come from the heart, enter the heart.

- Speak for their benefit, not yours: People are more likely to listen when they feel you're speaking with their best interests in mind. Avoid saying things just to advance your own agenda.

- Timing is everything. Not everything needs to be said immediately. Wait for the opportune time.

"No one cares how much you know unless they know how much you care"

Knowing that your partner always listens to you and understands what you are saying is a powerful tool for creating a strong relationship. Listening properly is a big step to help a couple get to the commitment phase of the relationship.

Read the Back of Your Shirt

You must be aware that as you are in the Research Phase of your relationship, the person you are dating is also evaluating you. Just as you're getting to know them, they're forming opinions about you—both the good and the not-so-good. This requires an honest look in the mirror to acknowledge that you, like everyone, have flaws, and some may even be outside your awareness.

Understanding your own faults is called self-awareness. Mike Zani, CEO of Predictive Index, offers a great way to think about this in his book The Science of Dream Teams.[3] He introduces an analogy he learned from a partner at Bain & Company, one of the big 3 consulting companies headquartered in Boston, Massachusetts.

Picture yourself wearing a shirt with writing on both the front and back. On the front of the shirt are all the great things people have said about you—qualities that you know about and are proud of. These are the parts of you that are easily visible to both yourself and others. But the back of the shirt has writing too—these are the traits, habits, or flaws that others notice, but you might not. These are your blind spots.

Self-awareness, then, is not just about knowing your strengths—it's about discovering and working on your weaknesses as well. This honesty, both with yourself and your partner, lays the groundwork for a more authentic connection.

To become more self-aware, it's essential to invite the people around us to help identify what's on the "back of our shirts." This candid feedback can illuminate aspects of ourselves we may not even realize that are impacting our relationships. Here are some common traits or behaviors that might be on the back of our shirt:

- Struggles to listen effectively
- Lacks awareness of others' needs
- Dominates or stands too close during conversations
- Dresses poorly or inappropriately
- Maintains poor hygiene or eating habits
- Socially awkward

These are just a few of the back of the shirt issues that people are unaware about.

People who truly want to improve their chances of an amazing relationship are willing to withstand the discomfort of candid feedback. They realize they have blindspots that need improving—and are willing to take that feedback to heart to improve.

If you don't take to heart what's on the back of your shirt, you may repeat the same mistakes over and over and not even realize there is a problem. Here are two effective ways to discover what areas you can improve upon:

Seek out feedback and critique. Don't surround yourself solely with people who tell you what you want to hear. Seek out people willing to tell you what you *need* to hear—people who will call out what's on the back of your shirt. It is always nice to have people who are your "yes men." These are usually your friends who are always on your side and will give you positive feedback about all your decisions in your life. You don't want "yes men" helping you to make decisions. You need people who will tell you the truth without any bias involved.

I went through this problem while trying to improve the writing of my books. Almost everyone who read one of them would tell me they liked them. Even though their views were appreciated, those were all biased opinions. Unless my writing was extremely poor (which it probably isn't, since you're still reading this far), they would probably like my books because they like me. I want to know everything that I can improve upon and all the mistakes that I *don't* know about. I want someone to tell me what is on the back of *my shirt.*

Accept Feedback Without Being Defensive. The next time someone gives you honest feedback, even if it is uncomfortable. Instead, just listen and thank them in the moment before taking the time to contemplate. Even if you don't agree with what they say, you have been given the gift of actually knowing how they feel. If you respond negatively or defensively, it will be the last time you get that honest feedback; no one will tell you again what's on the back of your shirt directly, they will just talk about it when you aren't around. Our first reaction to getting negative feedback is generally to give an excuse or rationalization of why their viewpoint is wrong. Your opinion may change later on when you had time to contemplate what they said. You then may then even agree with their criticism of you.

I've met many people struggling to find someone to date, and I try to be honest with them about why I think they are failing. Some take it personally and believe I'm wrong about what I see written on the back of their shirt. However, those who were willing to listen ended up finding success in their relationships. In fact, I once received a phone call on someone's wedding night, thanking me for helping them improve themselves and open their heart to love.

Case study: I was coaching a guy who was about 35 years old. He was very sweet, but did not have the greatest social skills. Unlike some older single men I meet, he wasn't a weirdo; he simply didn't have much experience talking to women, which made him nervous. Recognizing this, he sought coaching to improve.

Him: "Coach, I need some help. I went on one date with this woman and I think I want to marry her"

Me: "What? Are you sure?"

Him: "Yes coach. How can I get her to want to marry me?"

Me: "If you really want to lock her in, you have to show that you really like her. You have to be vulnerable so she knows that your heart is open."

I advised him to tell her on their second date that he really liked her, but in a way that felt sincere and heartfelt. So we practiced saying, 'You know, I really like you,' repeating it until he felt comfortable and natural. They ended up engaged by their eighth date, and now he's living happily ever after.

Case study: I met this man in one of my classes in Jerusalem. He was in his mid-40s and, from my perspective, could use some help. You can sometimes tell right away when someone is socially awkward—not just by their appearance, but by their overall demeanor. He was one of those individuals who struggled in social settings. He confided in me about his difficulty getting a second date, and I empathized with his frustration, so I agreed to help. Unfortunately, as we worked together, his challenges proved to be even deeper than I initially realized.

He began texting me multiple times a day, sending not just brief messages, but lengthy, rambling thoughts. It was as if he was pouring out all his internal reflections in each text.

When we met for coffee, I noticed that he couldn't hold eye contact, constantly looking away as if searching his mind for what to say next. It was like when someone giving a speech loses focus and glances upward to find their words—kind of like looking into their brain—except he did it nonstop, barely maintaining eye contact for more than a few seconds. I asked if he was aware of this habit, and he admitted he was, but had never tried to change it. I explained that on a date, if you can't keep eye contact on a woman, she's going to think you're nuts and you're unlikely to get a second chance. He seemed unaware that this was an issue. Unfortunately, he did nothing about it and his constant, long-winded texts eventually became so overwhelming that I had to block him.

This was a case of me reading him the back of his shirt, but him doing nothing about it.

Becoming more self-aware isn't meant to be comfortable. But what's far more uncomfortable is being the only person in the room unaware of the reality that's obvious to everyone else standing behind you. What you do with the information that someone gives you is entirely up to you. The guy that needed coaching to lock in this woman for marriage listened to my advice and got what he wanted. The other guy has not listened to my coaching and continues to have lots of first dates.

If Fortune 500 companies invest between $100 to $150 million a month in consulting services, it's clear that getting advice from an outside perspective improves their bottom line. In the realm of relationships, these "consultants" are marriage counselors—yet people typically only seek them when their relationship is unraveling. Ideally, people would seek advice from relationship consultants before entering the dating world. A good consultant can provide insights on what you need to do to increase your chances of finding a meaningful, lifelong partnership. Since this is rarely done, I hope this book will serve as your dating coach.

Consider how many people you know who have been dating for years without finding a long-term relationship. Now, imagine someone telling you everything they think is wrong with you. Would you truly listen and work on yourself, or would you dismiss their advice? If you've been dating for a long time with little success, it's possible no one has ever read the back of your shirt. If you want to get closer to the phase of Never Leaving, find someone honest enough to read it to you—and be open to listening.

Your Ego
is Not Your Amigo

Our ego may pose the greatest threat to the success of our relationships. The ego manifests itself in the car we drive, the house we live in, the titles we pursue, and even in the way we choose our partners—sometimes more for the attention they bring than for genuine connection. Consider, for example, the phenomenon of wealthy older men dating much younger women. In many cases, these relationships aren't about soulful connections, but are simply about boosting ones ego. They get their ego filled by walking into a restaurant with a woman on their arm who is 40 years younger. It's a way to fill the void left by low self-esteem. It reflects a need for validation and importance in the eyes of others. When we feel insecure, we may compensate by seeking ways to inflate our egos, attempting to appear more important.

One thing our ego likes to do is to make ourselves look good. Why? We feel good about ourselves when we're told we look good. Who doesn't like that? If you don't find that positive feedback from others, especially your partner, you may try to find something else to help you achieve that boost in your ego. It can be in the car you drive, jewelry, clothes, or how good you think your body looks. It can also be in your job title or how successful you want others to think you are. It can even manifest itself in something as simple as a purse.

Hermès makes a bag called the Birkin, which, despite being marketed as a tote, is essentially a high-end purse. The Diamond Himalaya Birkin is infamous for being the most expensive handbag ever sold. In 2022, Sotheby's sold a Diamond Himalaya Birkin 30 for over $450,000. Recently, prices for the most desirable non-diamond Himalaya Birkin 25 in store fresh condition is around $200,000.

Meanwhile, countless companies sell knockoffs, or ones that are similar in style that look almost identical for a fraction of the price. So, why would people pay such astronomical sums for a designer handbag when they could buy a similar-looking version for much less?

A friend of mine sells millions of dollars' worth of luxury purses each year. I asked him why people spend so much on Hermès bags, and he explained that they're considered valuable assets by the wealthy. Hermès also limits production, making the bags rare. Each purse is hand-stitched, and many are crafted from exotic materials like crocodile or alligator skin. But as we continued talking, he admitted that spending that much on a purse is, frankly, a bit absurd. Ultimately, he said, people buy Hermès bags because of ego. If it makes you feel good about yourself and you have the disposable income, go for it—just recognize that the purchase might be compensating for low self-esteem.

Having a passionate marriage is only achievable when your ego is not controlling your life. My friend mentioned that many of the Birkin bags he resells come from women going through divorce, which underscores my point: when the ego needs inflating—whether through buying expensive items or seeking validation—it can deflate the strength of a marriage.

I went through something similar when I was younger. I had always dreamed of owning a Porsche—not because it was practical or sensible, but because I thought I would look cool driving it. If I wanted practical, I would have purchased a Honda. I believed the car would elevate my status and self-image. So, in the mid-1990s, when I saved enough money, I bought a 1988 Porsche Cabriolet convertible. It was everything I had imagined, sexy and powerful—exactly the same way I thought of myself!

However, not long after purchasing the car, the thrill I had anticipated quickly turned to disappointment. I quickly figured that although the car was still great, I wasn't so sexy, nor was I so powerful. For anyone who has owned a high-end sports car, you know that the maintenance is expensive. From what I remember, it seemed that every time I walked into the repair shop, it would cost me a lot of money. Alternator broke? $1000. Out of alignment? $1000. Low air in tire? $1000. Okay, maybe that wasn't $1000, but that is what I remember.

While I had anticipated these costs, the stress of paying them far outweighed the pleasure I thought I would get from owning the Porsche.

This experience is the perfect metaphor for marriage. Everyone *knows* marriage is hard and requires lots of compromise and communication to stay in a passionate relationship. Everyone *knows* that even the best marriages will go through turbulence. When the pain of being in a marriage outweighs the pleasure, you get a divorce. It's the same with my Porsche—when the costs and headaches of repairs eclipsed the excitement, I sold the car.

The real lesson for me was that my desire to own the Porsche was entirely driven by my ego. The anticipation of owning it was far more thrilling than the actual ownership. This realization changed how I viewed many things in life. I learned that I didn't need the Porsche—I only wanted it to boost my self-image. I only wanted it for my ego!

If you think finding a husband or wife will magically make you happy or boost your ego, you may find yourself in the same situation I was in with my Porsche. The real purpose of a car is to get from point A to point B, which nearly any vehicle can do just as well. Similarly, the purpose of a marriage is not to elevate your social standing, but to build a meaningful connection with your partner.

Ego-driven desires—whether it's a fancy car, expensive clothes, or a big house—only serve to draw attention to ourselves. When the focus is on yourself rather than your spouse, problems will inevitably arise. If you can resist the urge to act on your ego, you can keep it in check and avoid letting it interfere with your chances of finding and keeping the love of your life. After all, as the saying goes, "Your ego is not your amigo."

You Must
Love Yourself

As you navigate the research phase of a potential relationship, it's crucial to ensure that the person you're considering sharing your life with genuinely loves themselves. This might seem unconventional, but if you think this person could be "the one," consider asking them directly. They may have never been posed this question, and it could reveal hidden wounds. At least with open wounds, you have a chance to heal them.

A common misconception is that personal issues will simply vanish once you find love. However, the truth, which may people do not want to accept, is that you must love yourself first to be open to loving someone else.

This is similar to using drugs to escape reality: it might work temporarily, but eventually, the high fades, and you're left facing your problems. If you marry someone with the hope that they will solve your issues or bring you happiness, you may find that not only do those problems persist, but you also risk making your partner unhappy, compounding your troubles. Before entering a relationship, you only have your own feelings to manage; in marriage, your emotions directly impact your spouse.

Someone committed to personal growth can learn from everyone they encounter, especially their partners. I've been fortunate to date some remarkable women, each teaching me valuable lessons, particularly about what not to do.

Unfortunately, I once dated someone who was extremely unhappy with herself. She had trust issues from her parents and that eventually caused major problems in our relationship. Early on I knew that she was a fantastic person and of course, when you first meet someone, unless they are totally nuts, you don't see the hidden dangers. So when I got past the Crush Phase and started the Research Phase, red flags began to appear.

I stopped dating her because I realized her unhappiness was a barrier to any future healthy relationship. Thankfully, after our relationship ended, she was able to seek help and come to terms with herself and her past. Looking back, I believe our relationship helped her to realize that she needed serious professional help. Even years ago, I knew that there had to be a Phase between the Crush phase and the Commitment Phase. This experience reinforced my belief in the importance of the Research Phase—understanding who you might be committing to is essential.

When I reached my mid-thirties and remained single, I made a conscious choice to prioritize my happiness, regardless of whether I got married. This mindset reduced the pressure of finding a spouse, making me more open to meeting the love of my life. It's easy to feel the weight of societal expectations, especially for women who may feel their biological clock ticking. Everyone faces unique personal challenges that they must confront in order to love others fully and allow themselves to be loved in return.

Regardless of your challenges, taking steps to love yourself and maintain a positive outlook will set you on the right path toward finding a partner with whom you can reach the point of "Never Leaving."

Happiness Is a Choice! Here are two effective strategies to cultivate happiness:

Focus on Your Blessings: Concentrate on what you have rather than what you lack. For instance, if you're reading this, you are blessed with the gift of sight. Imagine being blind your entire life and suddenly gaining the ability to see through a new procedure—how ecstatic would you feel? Cultivating this appreciation can help you attract a partner who values life as you do.

Spread Happiness to Others: There's nothing more fulfilling than bringing joy to someone else through kind words or actions. While self-indulgence may provide temporary satisfaction, it often lacks lasting fulfillment. In contrast, doing a good deed for someone else fosters a deep sense of well-being.

By focusing on your own happiness and spreading joy to others, you'll create a positive environment that attracts the right partner and paves the way for a healthy, loving relationship.

Defining Marriage

While any relationship is in the research phase, both parties must have a common understanding of what marriage means to them, especially if you want to get married or want to improve a current relationship.

What being married means to someone depends on their personal experience. Most of what people know about marriage comes from one source—their parents. This is why if you want your children to have a great marriage, you must show them what a great marriage is.

If you were fortunate enough to come from a home in which your parents had a healthy marriage, you had a positive experience and you will most likely try to emulate that. Conversely, if you were raised in a home with a dysfunctional or tumultuous marriage, those patterns may affect your own relationships. This doesn't mean you're destined to repeat history, but it does mean you must be mindful of the baggage and challenges you carry. Statistics show that children of divorced parents have a higher likelihood of divorcing themselves, especially for women.

Although divorce may be necessary in many instances (see Phase 3), if parents knew the harm that it will cause their children, we would see much less of it. It is fairly common to hear a couple who are getting divorced say that their children will be better off when they are separated. Although this may be true on the surface, what you won't hear them say is that their children may be internally damaged. Research shows that children are deeply affected by divorce, and the trauma can carry into their own adult relationships.

Before entering marriage, or if you're working on improving one, both partners should clarify their own definition of marriage. It's a mistake to assume that everyone shares the same understanding. At the very least, if you don't agree with what I consider to be the feeling and definition of marriage, it's essential for the couple to define their own terms of the meaning.

The Feeling of Marriage

The feeling of being married is when you feel complete as a person. It's when your primary purpose in life becomes giving to your spouse, with no lingering doubts that you might have "done better" with someone else. You know fully well that there are more attractive, wealthier, or emotionally healthier people out there, but none of that matters because you wouldn't trade your spouse for anyone else. Reaching this feeling doesn't happen overnight. It takes years of nurturing, learning, and growing together.

"The feeling of being married
is when you feel complete
as a person"

The Definition of Marriage

The definition of marriage is the merging of two souls. While many people use the analogy of marriage as a "team" or "partnership," I believe this analogy falls short. A team has a shared purpose—typically to win a game. But after winning a championship, a team often disbands or struggles to maintain the same success year after year. Unless you're someone like Tom Brady or Michael Jordan, leading a team to multiple championships is incredibly rare.

Since you are probably not the LeBron James or Serena Williams in your marriage, you will have to work harder to make your relationship into a dynasty. You want your marriage to win the championship every year!

A partnership is often when two people come together because each has something the other needs—usually resources or contacts. Once those goals are met, the partnership may lose its purpose, and the two might feel they no longer need each other. For example, in business, a partnership might be formed because one person lacks certain skills that the other provides; but once those skills are acquired, the need for the partnership fades. In a similar way, many marriages face strain or even end after children are born, as the initial goal—starting a family—has been fulfilled. If the focus of the marriage was solely on that goal, the connection between the spouses may weaken once it's achieved.

The danger in viewing marriage as a partnership is that it often leads to scorekeeping. Partners start to question whether the other is contributing equally, and how do you define "equal" in a marriage? Is it about who brings in the most money? Who takes care of the kids more? It's impossible to quantify these contributions. And when couples fall into this mindset, resentment builds, leading to breakdowns in the relationship.

Once someone's goals are achieved, one business partner may buy the other business partner out, or as often happens, end up suing each other in court. Partnerships can fall apart if one person feels that the other isn't contributing their fair share.

Viewing marriage as the merging of two souls means embracing unity, where you and your spouse are not separate, but truly one. Think about who you naturally love the most—likely, it's yourself. So when you give deeply to your spouse, they become an extension of yourself. There's an even more profound reason to see marriage this way: would you intentionally hurt yourself? While some may struggle with self-destructive tendencies, most people would never knowingly cause physical pain or hurl insults to themselves. In the same way, when you hurt your spouse, you're ultimately harming yourself.

> *"Your wife is complaining*
> *that her arm is hurting her.*
> *She has tried with no success*
> *to ease the pain.*
> *You go with her to the orthopedist*
> *to get some help.*
> *When you walk into the doctor's office,*
> *you say to the doctor,*
> *"our" arm hurts"*

There's a powerful lesson from the Bible that speaks to this: God put Adam to sleep and created a woman from one of his ribs, symbolizing that a spouse is meant to be the missing piece that completes us. The essence of marriage is not about two separate people, but about the union of two halves of a soul. It is through this merger that you become whole, emotionally and spiritually.

I believe that the person you choose to marry in your early 20s won't be the same person—nor will you—by the time you're 30, 40, or 50. As emotionally healthy individuals grow and evolve, I also believe there are many people you could potentially fall in love with and build an incredible marriage.

This is why comparing your spouse to someone else is always a losing game. Relationships thrive when we focus on what we have, not on what we don't have, or what might have been.

I often tell my wife that I wish I had met her 10 years earlier. She always responds, 'You weren't ready then.' And she's probably right—I would have passed her by because I was not mature enough to recognize how amazing she truly is.

Imagine ripping a heart-shaped piece of paper in half. One half represents you at birth, and the other half is out there, waiting to join with you. Together, these halves form one complete heart. That's the goal of marriage—to unite two souls into one heart and one life.

Ultimately, this is the key to a lasting, fulfilling marriage. It's not about being equal partners in a business transaction or striving to win a championship together. It's about becoming one with your spouse, loving them as an extension of yourself, and working together with a single mission and purpose in life. By focusing on the soul rather than the score, we can form one heart—one life together, that truly lasts a lifetime.

The Three Questions You Must Ask Before Getting Married

Young adults often ask me for advice when they feel unsure about whether they should marry the person they're currently dating. These three questions can provide valuable clarity and offer useful insights to guide you through the dating process.

Question 1
Am I Physically Attracted to This Person?

Physical attraction is undeniably important, and you need to feel a positive vibe to your partner's appearance. However, true attraction goes deeper than looks—it's about being drawn to their inner beauty as well. As discussed earlier in The Crush Phase, the more you truly get to know someone, the more attractive they become to you.

Conversely, the more flaws or negative traits you discover, the less appealing they may become, or what was at one time good-looking, is now ugly. Real, lasting attraction grows from a combination of physical connection and admiration for who they are on the inside.

Think back to the funniest guy or girl from your high school or college days. They were often dating someone who was quite attractive, even if they themselves weren't good-looking. Humor has a powerful way of making people feel good about themselves, and that can easily overshadow any lack of physical beauty. A great sense of humor can be just as magnetic, if not more so, than looks—it's a trait that makes people feel good and creates attraction.

You may be physically attracted to the person you will eventually marry, but that does not make them physically attractive. You might like someone who is an intellectual, a good listener, or someone who really understands you. Whatever initially attracts you, the more you get to know and appreciate them on a deeper level, the more attractive they'll become in your eyes. Ultimately, it doesn't matter what others think—you're the one who will share a life with this person.

This question that you should ask yourself is relatively straightforward, and most people will likely answer "yes." However, it's important to ask because if you're still in the Crush or Research Phase and are still struggling with their physical appearance, that feeling probably won't change over time. It could be an indication that this isn't the right match for you, and it may be a signal to move on.

Question 2

Do We Share
a Meaningful Purpose in Life?

Why is it so important to discuss your meaningful life purpose? Because most people invest more time planning their wedding day than their actual marriage. How long does the average wedding last? At the most, 5 hours. But a marriage is meant to last a lifetime. Unfortunately, without aligning on our meaningful purpose in life beforehand, the average marriage today lasts only about seven years. By having these conversations early, you set the foundation for a strong, lasting partnership, ensuring you're both working toward a shared future rather than just a great party.

Couples often dedicate an immense amount of time to planning their wedding day, obsessing over details like who makes the "A" list and which distant cousins won't get an invite. Then there's the reception to organize—choosing the caterer, photographer, band, color scheme, venue, date, and menu. Some brides even go to great lengths, traveling across the country to be fitted for an Oscar de la Renta gown or Christian Louboutin shoes that they'll only wear once. In fact, many brides spend more on a wedding dress than some people spend on their entire wedding! While these details may seem crucial in the moment, they pale in comparison to the significance of building a lasting marriage.

Is that truly where your priorities lie? A meaningful life extends far beyond choosing a beautiful wedding dress or planning an extravagant event. One of your first substantial conversations should be about the big picture—like your thoughts on children. How do you both envision parenting, and what values will guide your family? Next, consider how you'll spend your time together. Will you dedicate yourselves solely to leisure activities like vacations and sporting events, or do you plan to give back to others and help those in need?

What might seem unimportant now can become essential as life progresses. Set a foundation by discussing these deeper priorities early on—this will ensure your relationship grows with a meaningful purpose.

"You are on vacation in New York City on a sightseeing boat touring around Manhattan. Suddenly you see a young boy fall overboard. You scream for help, but everyone around you is immobilized and panicked. You jump in to save the boy yourself and with help from the crew, you are able to get him back onboard. The boy is crying, but physically unharmed. You're exhausted and traumatized, but thrilled that you were able to save a life. You go back to your hotel room and shower off all the muck from the Hudson River and fall down on the bed, exhausted. After many years and countless vacations all over the world, which vacation do you think will be the most memorable?"

If it's not the vacation where you saved a young boy, you might have some work to do! Few things add more meaning to life than saving someone's life—especially a child's. A sense of purpose and meaning is essential in a relationship, and these are the moments we truly cherish in the long run.

In Stephen Covey's bestselling book, The 7 Habits of Highly Effective People, habit #2 encourages us to "start with the end in mind." While you might expect this advice to apply to business success—like planning what to do with your company when you retire, whether to sell, pass it on to your children, or take it public—Covey is actually referring to something far deeper. He challenges us to think about our legacy after we're gone—not just in business, but in life. What values will you leave behind? How will people remember you? Covey emphasizes that true success lies in shaping the meaningful impact you leave on others, not just your professional achievements.

He prompts us to ask ourselves a powerful question: "What do you want people to say at your funeral?" This reflection helps clarify what truly matters in your life. If you accumulate wealth, do you want to be remembered for your expensive cars and lavish homes? Would you prefer to be eulogized as a hard worker who sacrificed weekends and family time for the sake of your career? Or would you rather be celebrated for the meaningful moments spent with family and friends, as well as your philanthropic efforts throughout your life? It's unlikely that anyone said on their deathbed that they wished to have worked more hours. Instead, what most people cherish are the connections they made and the positive impact they had on others.

No one ever says on his deathbed,
"I wished I worked more hours"

When your life centers around a meaningful purpose rather than just accumulating wealth, you'll likely find that your marriage—and life in general—becomes more fulfilling and significant as well. Learning to be a giver can significantly enhance your relationships, as love flourishes by the act of giving. Remember our earlier discussion about the feeling of being in love? It's about giving to someone without expecting anything in return. If giving to others helps us feel that way, maybe we should even give to others that are *not* our spouse. How much more pleasure and meaning would we get in life. It's this common purpose that will drive the pleasure in our relationship.

Ultimately, there are only two legacies you leave behind: your children and your deeds. Your deeds represent what you accomplished in your lifetime, while your children embody your values and beliefs. Strive to leave a legacy that inspires them to carry on generosity and kindness.

Be careful of confusing common purpose with having common interests—like hobbies or favorite activities. Sure, it's nice if both of you enjoy the music of Maroon 5 and like watching Breaking Bad. These things can make dating more enjoyable, but they're not the foundation for a lasting relationship. If you want someone to enjoy your hobbies with, that's what friends are for! While having common interests with your partner is great, it's not the "secret ingredient" that leads to a lifelong relationship.

Back in the 1980s and '90s, when I lived in the Washington, DC area, you couldn't escape hearing about the Washington Redskins (now the Commanders). They won three Super Bowls in 10 years, and the entire region was obsessed with the team.

When I dated women back then, I often asked if they enjoyed watching Redskins games. Almost all said yes.

But after getting to know them better, it became clear most of them didn't care about football at all—they said yes because they thought that sharing my interest would make me happy.

Early in a relationship, having common interests might seem important, but years into marriage, those interests often fade into the background. Once life gets busier with work, marriage, and children, do couples still spend time watching football, working out together, or playing softball like they used to? Often, much less. Common interests might help you find someone, but they won't sustain a marriage.

Common interests may be the reason that you end up finding someone to marry, but to get to "Never Leaving", you need a lot more than a cruise to the Bahamas, playing Scrabble and Pilates. What truly holds a marriage together is not shared hobbies, but shared meaningful purpose.

To illustrate this, let's revisit an example from earlier in this book—the cooking show Chopped. There was an episode where the competition paired up four couples on blind dates. Each couple had to work together as a team to create the best dish and win the grand prize. Typically, out of 4 blind dates, it would be unusual for more than one couple to hit it off and want another date. Just think about if you set up 4 blind dates with the singles you know. What are the chances that even one of them would go out again? Maybe one, if you're lucky. In this instance. All 4 couples wanted to date again privately.

So, why did all four couples want a second date? It's because they shared a meaningful purpose—even if, in this case, it was simply cooking a dish for the judges. Working toward a common objective gave them a sense of connection.

Now, imagine how much stronger a relationship could be if the shared purpose was something far more significant than winning a cooking competition. When couples share a meaningful life purpose—whether it's raising a family, contributing to their community, or supporting each other's dreams—it provides a deeper bond than just enjoying the same music or movies. This shared purpose is what truly keeps a relationship thriving long after the initial excitement fades.

To get to "Never Leaving," you need more than shared interests. You need a meaningful shared purpose.

Why Do You Need a Shared Meaningful Life Purpose in Life?

Why is having a shared meaningful life purpose so essential to a lasting relationship? Because one of the greatest feelings in life is having a sense of meaning and purpose. Knowing that you are needed and that your life has a direction brings a deep sense of fulfillment. Couples who share a meaningful life purpose are far more likely to stay together, as their relationship is rooted in something deeper than fleeting passions or external factors.

Purpose is often forward-looking—it's about where you're headed and what you hope to achieve. Meaning, on the other hand, is backward-looking—it's built on what you've accomplished and the role you've played in your life so far. When you have purpose, that creates meaning. Together, purpose and meaning create a foundation that transcends the physical world. This is why relationships built on purely physical factors, like attraction or financial success, are often more likely to fail. These things don't last, and once they fade, couples can find themselves disconnected.

Beyond the Physical

It's crucial that your shared meaningful purpose isn't based solely on physical desires. Take, for instance, the goal of having children. While raising a family is a noble and fulfilling life goal, it can't be the only thing binding you together. What happens when the children grow up and leave the house? Many couples experience a sense of emptiness when they no longer have the day-to-day responsibilities of raising kids and they may find they've lost touch with one another. You may have a couple whose children have moved out of the house and are now staring at each other in the kitchen wondering why they got married in the first place! This often leads to "empty-nest" divorces. While raising children is deeply fulfilling, a truly meaningful life together needs to go beyond that.

The same holds true for couples who focus their shared goals on material success—whether it's building wealth, buying a big house, or taking luxury vacations. While these can certainly make life more comfortable, they can't sustain a relationship. Once the thrill of accumulating wealth or the excitement of a fancy vacation wears off, couples may find themselves asking, "What now?" They risk becoming like those who spend their days obsessed with external pleasures—whether that's choosing the right designer outfit or driving your Bentley to your country club. Then your sole purpose may be spending 4 hours chasing a little white ball into a small hole in as few shoots as possible. The whole time you are wondering why you were married in the first place!

Wealth Doesn't Guarantee Success

Recently, we've seen some of the world's wealthiest individuals, like Jeff Bezos and Bill Gates, go through very public divorces. These examples highlight the fact that money doesn't necessarily make a relationship easier. In fact, it can introduce its own set of challenges. Some might even argue that poverty can foster a stronger bond, as couples work together to survive and pay the bills. When money is no longer a worry, new challenges arise—competing priorities, distractions, or even a loss of purpose.

It's telling that wealthier cities often have a higher concentration of divorce attorneys. Money, while making life more comfortable, does not guarantee a long-lasting, loving relationship. So, it's important to understand that financial success is not a meaningful life purpose that will sustain your marriage.

Common Interests Aren't Enough

Some couples bond over shared physical activities, like working out, running, or playing sports together. While staying healthy is important, making physical fitness the central focus of your relationship can also lead to problems. What happens when your body can't keep up with the same exercise routine as you age, or when life's demands—like raising children or managing careers—get in the way of your fitness goals? If your relationship is based solely on working out together, it can begin to fall apart when those activities take a back seat.

Personally, I used to run with my wife when we were dating. But now, with kids and other responsibilities, our workout sessions together are rare. While physical fitness remains important, it's not the central pillar of our relationship—and that's okay.

Physical intimacy, however, is critical to a strong marriage. A loving, physical connection must be a regular part of the relationship. Without it, the marriage will deteriorate.

Yet, even this essential component needs to be coupled with something deeper. A marriage based solely on physical factors—whether it's children, wealth, or fitness—will struggle in the long run.

The kids finally leave the house, you've amassed great wealth, you are a top-rated marathon runner or have a killer body at 50. Now what is your marriage based on? There must be *something more.*

So What's Next?

The answer lies in finding a shared meaningful life purpose—something that transcends the physical world and gives both of you a sense of direction. Whether it's building a legacy, contributing to a cause, or nurturing a deep spiritual connection, this shared purpose will serve as the glue that holds your relationship together. It's this sense of shared meaning that can take a relationship from good to the unbreakable 4th phase, Never Leaving.

Your shared meaningful life purpose must be rooted in something deeper than just the physical world. By either incorporating spirituality or a passion for a cause, you create a foundation that can withstand external pressures. Without this, your net worth becomes your self-worth. You will both have a sense of fulfillment that transcends material success, helping both of you remain content and centered, regardless of life's ups and downs.

> *"Without spirituality,*
> *your net worth*
> *becomes your self-worth"*

Case study: A non-profit organization once invited me to attend a major donor event in Miami. At the time, I was working in Los Angeles and I was not planning to go. Alas, they offered me a ride on a donor's private jet from Los Angeles to Miami. With a smile, I agreed.

At the small airport, I met the jet's owners—an older couple with no children. I was immediately struck by how passionate they were together. While they clearly enjoyed the luxury of private jet travel, they also dedicated much of their resources to supporting non-profits aligned with their values, which were mainly conservative political organizations. Beyond financial contributions, they actively advised these organizations on how to achieve lasting success.

What stood out most was the strength of their marriage, which they attributed to sharing a deep, meaningful purpose. Their partnership was built on a foundation of making a positive impact in the world.

Here are eight characteristics to look for in someone that may have a shared meaningful purpose with you:

1. **Commitment to Growth:** They actively seek ways to grow both personally and spiritually. They understand that life is a journey of continuous learning and self-improvement.

2. **Service to Others:** Always on the lookout for opportunities to contribute, they don't wait for someone to ask for help—they anticipate the needs of others and step in willingly.

3. **Kindness to All:** Whether it's a waiter or a celebrity, they treat everyone with respect and dignity. Their compassion extends to all people, regardless of status.

4. **Positive Judgment:** They approach others with an open mind, choosing to see the good and judging people favorably, even when it's difficult.

5. **Contentment:** They are happy with what they have, and they don't constantly strive for more material possessions. Their happiness comes from within, not from external circumstances.

6. **Big-Picture Thinker:** They avoid getting caught up in small, trivial details. Instead, they see the bigger picture and are able to step back, allowing life to flow without trying to control every aspect.

7. **Doesn't Keep Score:** They don't measure the give-and-take in relationships. There's no tally of who did what, because love is not transactional to them.

8. **No Celebrity Worship:** They do not place undue importance on celebrities, athletes, or anyone in the public eye. Their role models are people of integrity and character, not those celebrated for superficial achievements.

So if you can answer "Yes" to the 2nd question, do we share a common meaningful purpose, you are on the path to having a passionate, loving relationship.

Question 3

For a Man:
Am I Willing To Make Her Happy for The Rest of My Life?

This question is directed specifically to men, and you'll understand why when you see the third question intended for women. The reason this question is not aimed at women is simple: when a man makes his wife happy, she'll want to make him happy.

If you can answer "Yes" to this question, you're well on your way to having an incredible marriage. It's important to envision your potential spouse not just as they are now, but as they might be twenty, thirty, or even forty years later in life. The demands of raising children, managing household responsibilities, and pursuing careers can take a toll on individuals, both physically and mentally. Moreover, as we age, the effects of time and gravity can lead to changes in our physical appearance that even the best aerobics or yoga routines can't completely counteract. To put it bluntly, you have to imagine your spouse 50 pounds heavier and still answer this question with a resounding "Yes!"

Although my wife and I are now in our 50s and certainly not in the same shape we were on our wedding day, I find her even more attractive than she was 24 years ago. Our meaningful life purpose aligns beautifully, and I've learned that the more I do things to make her happy, the more she wants to make me happy. If you can't envision wanting to support your spouse after they've gained weight or are facing emotional challenges, then Houston, we have a problem.

If you genuinely believe you would be willing to go over and beyond to support your spouse's happiness, you're on the right track. However, it's essential to agree on what "happiness" means to both of you before tying the knot. For instance, while a husband buying a kegerator for his wife might bring him joy, it will not do the same for her, unless she drinks a lot of beer. Clear communication about your definitions of happiness and how to achieve it together is crucial for building a strong, lasting marriage.

Question 4

For a Woman: Do I Respect My Future Husband?

Do you genuinely admire your potential husband for their abilities, qualities, and achievements? If you can't confidently answer "yes" to that question, it's time to reconsider. Respect is fundamental in any marriage. You can't say, "I'll only respect them if they improve their flaws or get a better job." You must accept your partner for who they are, as it's likely they won't change significantly after marriage. If you're not happy with them now, chances are you won't be happy later. While your future spouse may express a willingness to improve, it's important not to rely solely on that promise. True compatibility comes from appreciating and respecting each other as you are, right now. Of course, a husband must also respect his wife, but it is just something that's more important for a male to feel.

Let's consider a scenario where you believe your future husband engages in some immature activities—like spending hours in his basement playing with electric trains. If this bothers you now, it's unlikely that those feelings will simply vanish after marriage. If you expect that he will abandon this hobby once you're married, you may find yourself disappointed. It's essential to recognize that this is how he enjoys spending his free time, and respecting his interests is crucial. Accepting each other's hobbies and quirks is a key part of building a healthy relationship.

Suppose your potential husband wants to go to law school so he can become a partner at a major law firm. This ambition will likely involve long hours of studying and busy weekends, leaving less time for family. He may expect you to handle household responsibilities alone while he focuses on his studies. If you choose to marry him, it's essential to respect his decisions and priorities.

You need to weigh your spouse's positive and negative character traits and decide if the relationship is worthwhile. People have the potential for personal growth as they get older, but only if they are honest and willing to do so. Be careful of inflexibility because that will keep them from improving themselves. Inflexibility can be a good quality when dealing with someone's morals, but not when it negatively affects the relationship.

Before I got married, watching football was incredibly important to me. In fact, I forgot to check the football schedule when we chose our wedding date. As luck would have it, the Washington Redskins had a game scheduled at the exact time of our wedding! So I did what any real football fan would do, I cancelled the wedding.

Of course, I didn't cancel the wedding to watch the game—far from it! In fact, I didn't even think about the game on that day. What mattered far more was that I was participating in an event of deep significance. I used to be inflexible about missing games, but I quickly learned that when something is truly meaningful, it eclipses everything else in your life. This experience taught me that love and commitment can create a sense of fulfillment that far surpasses any sporting event.

In many of my private coaching sessions, young women often share that they feel unsure about marrying the man they're dating. I ask them directly, 'Do you respect him?' If they hesitate or avoid eye contact, it's a clear sign that an underlying issue is troubling them.

Case Study: I was coaching a very sharp 24 year old young lady who been dating her boyfriend for several years. She was passionately bragging about him, so I asked her why she was meeting with me. She admitted that she was bothered by what she considered his lack of intelligence. I told her that he sounded fantastic and I even mentioned to her I'd like to meet him. When I eventually did, I found him just as she'd described—a great guy, though perhaps not the sharpest tool in the shed—he definitely was a bit slow. I encouraged her to try to make the relationship work because he really was a special guy with flawless character traits. A few months later, she called me in tears. She was struggling with the relationship and feeling conflicted. I asked her a direct question: "Do you respect him?" Her answer was, "No." I told her gently, "He will make a wonderful husband for someone—just not for you." She then asked me if she could date him for 2 more years until she finishes college. I told her that would not be very nice to him. I don't know what happened in the end.

When you're a young and single guy, respect might not be something you think much about or consider essential from a future spouse. But as you grow, respect becomes vital—it's essential for a man to feel respected, and lacking it should be a deal-breaker.

Although my future wife may have respected me, except my love of football, she recognized my willingness and ability to grow as a person. She saw potential in me that others overlooked. If you genuinely respect your spouse, you may find it easier to overlook certain character flaws, especially if you believe they have the potential for growth.

It's essential to distinguish between things you don't respect that are true deal-breakers, and those where compromise is possible. You must have genuine respect for your partner's character, intellect, emotions, and everything about them! When you respect your future spouse deeply, you lay a strong foundation for a lasting marriage—one where commitment is unwavering. As you navigate your relationship, ask yourself: Do I respect this person in every way possible? That's a question worth asking.

Body, Soul or Poke Bowl

What is a poke bowl? Essentially, it's deconstructed sushi—a combination of rice, vegetables like avocado and cucumbers, fresh fish (often salmon), and a flavorful sauce like soy or teriyaki. If you only have a bowl of rice, is that considered a poke bowl? No. What about just a bowl of salmon? Still no. It takes all the ingredients coming together to create a true poke bowl.

Humans are much the same. At our core, we're made up of three essential parts: body, ego, and soul. Focusing on just one while neglecting the others often leaves us falling short of our full potential. This imbalance can also create challenges in our relationships. Like the poke bowl, true harmony comes when all the pieces work together.

When you recognize that we are composed of three parts—body, ego, and soul—it reveals our inherently spiritual nature. Your body makes decisions on whether something feels good to you. Your ego makes decisions based on whether something looks good on you, and your soul makes decisions based on *what* is truly good for you.

This is a test with live with every day of our life, to try to choose our soul over our body or ego.

Google defines "spiritual" as something "affecting the human spirit as opposed to material or physical things." For the purposes of this book, let's break down the word spirituality into two parts: spirit and ritual.

Spirit: This represents the non-physical part of us—the essence of who we are. It includes our soul, our thoughts, and our ego. Though abstract, these qualities are fundamental to our being. Just because we can't see them doesn't make them any less real. Science has long explained the existence of invisible forces like air, radio waves, and gravity. Likewise, our spirit is an unseen force that drives us, shaping our values and how we connect with others.

Ritual: This is the physical side of our existence—the part we see and experience through our bodies. Rituals involve our daily habits and the routines that sustain us, like eating, breathing, and taking care of our basic needs. We often perform these actions without a second thought, but they are an essential part of our lives. The "ritual" component of spirituality represents the disciplined, purposeful actions we engage in to nourish our spiritual well-being.

Together, spirit and ritual make up the concept of spirituality. It's about understanding and nurturing both the unseen, eternal part of who we are, and the daily practices that bring those deeper values into our physical lives.

Focusing Beyond the Physical

When you first meet someone, it's natural to focus on their physical appearance—it's the first thing you notice and why I call it First Date Bias. If you base your relationship solely on what's visible, you risk missing out on a deeper connection, one that could last a lifetime. Too much emphasis on physical attraction can cause us to overlook potential soulmates, people whose spirit resonates with ours.

A spiritually grounded relationship encourages you to look beyond surface-level qualities and build a connection based on shared values and purpose. This deeper bond is what keeps relationships strong through the inevitable changes life brings. Whether it's aging, financial stress, or difficult challenges, spirituality can act as a constant, ensuring that your relationship isn't derailed—one that has the power to last through anything.

Understanding the Body & Soul

When preparing for marriage, it's crucial to recognize that your shared meaningful life purpose should extend beyond the physical realm and encompass spiritual fulfillment. This begins with the understanding that you, as a person, consist of both a body, ego and soul. If your soul lacks purpose or spiritual connection, you may attempt to fill that void by overindulging your body—seeking temporary satisfaction through physical means.

This compensatory behavior often manifests in various ways: focusing exclusively on your children, obsessing over physical fitness, accumulating wealth, taking extravagant vacations, or acquiring material possessions. Here's the key realization: your body will never be fully satisfied. The desires of the physical are insatiable, continually seeking more unless they are balanced by the fulfillment of your soul's deeper, spiritual desires.

Consider the last time you finished a can of Pringles or a bag of Doritos. After eating the final chip, were you truly satisfied? Probably not, because the craving for something salty or indulgent rarely goes away. Our physical selves are wired for cravings and can easily become addicted to fleeting pleasures. From a young age, we are conditioned to desire "more"—the better toy, the faster bike, the bigger house, the higher-paying job, the flashier car. When the body's desires dominate, it becomes increasingly difficult to find lasting satisfaction in anything, including marriage.

The body naturally seeks pleasure and gratification, which is why it often dictates our choices. Without a strong spiritual foundation, this tendency can lead us astray, driving us to make impulsive decisions that may feel good in the moment, but don't serve us in the long term. Take, for instance, the temptation of a delicious piece of chocolate cake. Our initial reaction is to indulge, perhaps even to have another slice if it's particularly rich and moist. But when do we stop? Do we stop when we're truly satisfied? Or do we stop only when we start feeling sick or guilty for overindulging?

The truth is, unless we learn to control our physical desires, we can easily fall into patterns of excess—whether it's overeating, overspending, or overindulging in any number of temporary pleasures. This lack of self-control can make it harder to maintain a balanced, fulfilling marriage. Relationships, just like our health, thrive on discipline and intentional choices. Without the ability to reign in your urges, you may find yourself becoming more reactive, more easily upset, and ultimately less connected to your partner on a deeper level.

To cultivate a meaningful, lasting relationship, you need to strike a balance between your body's needs, your ego's desire's and your soul's nourishment. Only when the soul is provided with spiritual meaning can you temper the body's cravings and build a life grounded in purpose, rather than fleeting pleasures.

Here are 3 scenarios that may help you to distinguish between the body and the soul, showing how they each manifest within us:

Scenario 1:

Imagine your friends are over to watch a football game. Your best friend Joey arrives and you tell him to grab a beer from the kitchen. Moments later, he collapses on the kitchen floor from a massive heart attack. Despite your efforts to revive him, the paramedics arrive and declare Joey dead. As they prepare to take his body away, your friend Matty arrives. You tearfully tell him, "Joey's gone." In shock, Matty runs to the kitchen, sees Joey's body lying on the floor, and exclaims, "What do you mean he's gone? He's right here!" You try to explain that Joey has died and that he is gone. Matty continues to argue with you and says, "Joey's not gone, he is right here."

The question you need to ask yourself is simple: Is Joey there, or is he not there? If you understand that included in our essence is a body and a soul, the answer becomes clear. However, if you don't recognize this, you may struggle to answer because your mind is caught in contradiction. This contradiction highlights a fundamental truth: Joey's body may be present, but his soul—the essence of who he was—is no longer there. The body and soul are distinct, and the real Joey departed with his soul.

Scenario 2:

You order a pizza with your favorite toppings. After three slices, you're full, but you notice there's one slice left. You wrestle with the temptation to eat it, and finally, you give in. After you enjoy eating the slice for about 30 seconds, you immediately feel awful—stuffed, uncomfortable, and filled with regret. You enjoyed the pizza in the moment, but the pleasure was fleeting. The guilt, however, lingers much longer.

This scenario illustrates how listening to the body over the soul often leads to short-lived gratification, followed by regret. Your body is unhappy because your stomach hurts, plus your soul is unhappy because it knows you made the wrong choice.

Scenario 3:

You've just completed a grueling 10-mile race. When you return home, you devour three sandwiches and collapse on the couch, exhausted and sore. Your body aches, and you can barely move, but how do you feel? You feel incredible! Why? Because even though your body is in pain, your soul is elated from finishing a 10 mile run. The joy of finishing the race far outweighs the physical discomfort. This is a clear example of how the soul's fulfillment brings a deeper, longer-lasting sense of satisfaction than the body's temporary cravings.

In Scenario #1, Joey's body remains, but his soul—his true essence—is gone. It's the only time we exist in two places: the body stays behind, but the soul moves on. In Scenarios #2 and #3, you can see that when the body is in control, lasting happiness is elusive, but when the soul takes charge, even in the face of discomfort or pain, you find joy and fulfillment. When you listen to your soul, you're more resilient, more accomplished, and much happier overall.

Following your soul allows you to rise above life's pettiness. A person who lives spiritually finds meaning even in challenges, recognizing them as opportunities for growth. This mindset is what true resilience looks like. It also dramatically improves relationships. Minor quirks or irritations that may have once bothered you about your spouse will no longer carry the same weight. Someone who is connected with their soul is better equipped to handle marriage's inevitable ups and downs.

When you live with a focus on your soul, you gain a deeper understanding of what it means to be in a lasting relationship—one where you are "Never Leaving." The love I have for my wife today, after 23 years of marriage, is profoundly deeper than when we first got married. This transformation is because we have both grown spiritually and have become less attached to material things. We've learned that all the possessions are ultimately meaningless. In fact, the more I acquired, the more I had to manage.

Everyone has quirks or habits that can be challenging in a marriage. The key is finding a partner who is committed to living with meaning and purpose, focusing on your positive traits and connecting with you on a spiritual level, beyond the physical. Now, with our focus on spirituality, I can devote the time and energy needed to nurture our relationship and help it flourish. Our **B**ody wants to do what feels good. Our **E**go wants to do what looks good. Our **S**oul wants to do what is good. This is the **T**est we live with every day, and focusing on your soul, especially in a relationship, is how we can be our *B-E-S-T*.

Phase 3

The
Commitment

The Commitment Phase begins once you've completed the Research Phase in your relationship. At this point, you've found no major deal-breakers that would prevent you from moving forward toward a lifelong partnership. However, it's important to remember that many challenges in marriage only surface years later, except the ones that surface while you're cutting the wedding cake. This is why it's essential to have a clear understanding of what love and marriage truly mean. You've also recognized that your feelings are more than just infatuation—they are rooted in genuine love. Reaching this phase may not have come from a single "aha" moment, but rather through a series of experiences and realizations that have guided you here.

Everything in this phase serves as the baseline necessary to even get close to the Never Leaving Phase of a relationship. This chapter should be considered essential reading for anyone contemplating tying the knot. It provides critical insights and understanding needed to build a lasting, committed marriage.

Sunscreen Love

Picture this: you're enjoying a weekend at your beach house. Before heading out, you diligently apply SPF 30 sunscreen to protect your skin. You spend the entire day at the beach, soaking up the sun and having a blast. But when you return to your beach house, step into the shower, and catch a glimpse of yourself in the mirror—you're completely sunburned. What happened?

You forgot to reapply the sunscreen.

Love works the exact same way.

As you walk down the aisle to merge two lives together, *every bride and groom* is thinking that they will be in love forever. You *think* love comes easy—because, at this moment, it does. Here is where the challenge lies, just like being on the beach when you are so busy swimming, walking, reading a book, taking a nap, you *completely forget* to reapply the sunscreen. It's no different than love, it's easy to forget that it also needs to be attended to.

Life gets busy—with careers, hobbies, and especially children—all of which can draw attention away from your relationship. Romancing the relationship means transforming that initial infatuation and desire into lasting love. If you don't, your relationship may suffer, just as you can get burned by forgetting to reapply sunscreen at the beach.

I've heard from men in their 40s and 50s who were shocked to receive divorce papers from their wives' attorneys, completely blindsided by the news. In many cases, they had lost sight of the importance of nurturing and maintaining the love.

If you don't consistently nurture and care for your relationship, the love you share can begin to fade, just as sunscreen does over time. Lasting love requires ongoing effort and renewal to keep it strong and resilient.

Many things can be mistaken for love: desire, infatuation, lust, and physical attraction. While these elements may spark a relationship, they are merely the tools that lead to true love. Romance, however, is the ongoing effort that sustains it—it's the continuous "reapplication of sunscreen" that keeps love alive. In the early stages of a relationship, romance doesn't feel like work because it flows naturally. But after living with someone for 10, 20 or even 30 years, it takes conscious effort. To keep love alive, you have to be willing to invest in romancing the relationship, even when it no longer feels effortless.

When you meet someone new, your focus is naturally on your own needs. You're likely not thinking, "I want to date so I can fulfill someone else's emotional, intellectual, and physical needs." Instead, you're considering what you're getting from the relationship, not what you can give. This is perfectly natural—true selflessness usually emerges only when real love develops. Only then do you begin to genuinely desire to give to someone else without expecting anything in return.

There is a certain amount of enthusiasm when dating. Everything is new and the unknown future is sometimes more exciting than the true reality. Once you get to the Commitment Phase, much of the mystery fades, and that's what may take the excitement level down a few notches. It may be that the original exhilaration we had fueled some of that desire that we had for someone early on. This is why we need to understand that love takes constant maintenance. It is not a given that because you loved someone at one time that it will continue forever. If that was the case, there would be almost no divorce!

> *"It is not a given*
> *that because you loved someone*
> *at one time that it will continue forever.*
> *If that was the case,*
> *there would be almost no divorce!"*

So how do we keep love in the marriage? The first step is to realize that it can't come by itself. There is an effort to acquire love, and that is romance. Romance is the behavior through which someone expresses their intimate feelings and emotions towards another person. Infatuation, lust, and desire are just the starting points—but they're not love. True love begins to grow when you add romance, transforming those initial feelings into something deeper. Romance isn't reserved for dating; it's an essential part of marriage and the key to reach the phase of Never Leaving.

> *"There is an effort to acquire love,*
> *and that is romance.*
> *Romance is the behavior through which*
> *someone expresses their intimate feelings*
> *and emotions towards another person"*

It is the act of showing your love for someone else. It is the little things you do on an ongoing bases. Touching, hugging, brushing up against them, writing love notes, spending quality time together, words of affection—these are all examples of romance. You must be showing romance to your spouse, and you also must be receiving it in a positive way. It is important to know your spouse's love language so that you can express the love in the way that makes them feel loved.

The most profound demonstration of real love can often be seen in older couples in their eighties. By this stage, the lust and physical desire have faded; the physical aspect of their relationship is no longer the main focus. Yet, their devotion and care for one another remain unwavering. They may not look the same as they did in their twenties—unless it's Cher—as the tools of lust have served their purpose in earlier years. Perhaps that's why God designed us to be attractive when we're young—to draw in the opposite gender and cultivate the lust and desire that ultimately leads to lasting love.

You've likely come across stories of elderly individuals caring for a spouse with Alzheimer's, even when that spouse no longer remembers them. Why do they do this? It exemplifies true love—not focusing on what one can gain from the relationship, but rather on what one can give. This is also reflected in the way we feel about friends who have passed away. Even if we didn't visit them during their illness, we often feel compelled to attend their funeral. They may not know we're there, but our presence is a testament to the love we felt for them. It's a selfless act, giving our time and support without expecting anything in return—an ultimate gesture of love.

Love requires effort and ongoing attention, much like applying sunscreen. Don't take for granted that it will endure without consistent nurturing. Just as neglecting to reapply sunscreen can lead to painful sunburn, failing to prioritize romance in your relationship can cause your relationship to burn. And unlike a sunburn, the loss of love can have far deeper consequences for which no amount of aloe will help you.

Compliment, Don't Criticize

I grew up in a home where criticism was common—often directed at me and my siblings. It may have been passed down from my parents' upbringing, where it was simply a part of their way of communicating. No one saw it as a negative trait at the time. The problem arises when criticism becomes so ingrained that it shapes who you are. You may not even realize you're being critical, and if you're married, one spouse may begin to resent the other. This can set off a downward spiral in the relationship, where it feels almost impossible to recover.

Think about how many times you may have criticized your spouse without even thinking about it. No one likes to be criticized. Every time you criticize your spouse, you are wiping the sunscreen off, and every time you compliment your spouse, you are putting sunscreen on. Understanding this concept can keep your relationship from burning.

Case study: I was coaching a woman in her late 30s—beautiful, accomplished, and with so much going for her. She shared with me about a recent, brief relationship that had just ended. Her story highlighted for me how common criticism can be in relationships.

She told me that she met her date at a restaurant, where they both ordered soup and sandwiches. As an observant Jew, she went to wash her hands and say a blessing before eating her bread, as is the custom for religious Jews. Her date, who was not nearly as observant, returned from washing his hands and started eating his sandwich without saying anything.

She then says to him, "Aren't you going to say a blessing?"

He responds, "No. I was just washing my hands because they were dirty."

She says, "You know, you're supposed to say a blessing before you eat your sandwich."

He then poured his soup all over her lap.

After she shared this story, I said to her, "Do you realize that you criticized him?"

She look surprised and responded, "No I didn't. I just want him to be a better man."

At this point, I told her, "You criticized him, and no one—man or woman— wants to be criticized!"

Are there times when criticism is necessary in a marriage? Absolutely. But far less often than you might think. For example, when your spouse leaves their underwear on the floor? Definitely not worth criticizing. Or when they forget to put the toilet seat down? Not even close. These minor inconveniences are easy to live with.

Think of it this way: when you criticize your spouse, it's like wiping sunscreen off someone at the beach. You're erasing the love and romance you've built, leaving your marriage exposed to the harsh rays of negativity. Most people don't take criticism well, and even though you are only criticizing an action, many people will take that as you being critical of them, and not the action.

Men, in particular, don't like being criticized because they often internalize it as a lack of respect. Some women tell me that their husbands do nothing around the house, and they can't stand it, so they criticize them. My advice to these women is to treat their husbands like a man they respect. When you do, you'll start to see them become a man that you respect. Find one thing, no matter how small, to compliment your husband on. You'll be surprised how much they appreciate the positive reinforcement, and hopefully, it will inspire them to seek more opportunities to earn your praise.

Before criticizing, take a moment to pause and ask yourself if it truly needs to be said. Instead of focusing on the negative, practice constructive communication. Frame your feedback by telling your spouse what you'd like them to do, rather than pointing out what you don't want. Focus on the positives. Remember, there was a reason you married this person—reconnect with that reason and you'll be more likely not to criticize.

Now, let's explore four key strategies to help keep the sunscreen on in your relationship, protecting and nurturing it for the long term.

The 4 A's: Attention, Affection, Appreciation & Awareness

Men and women often connect in different ways, and recognizing these differences is essential in building a deeper connection. In Gary Chapman's bestselling book, The Five Love Languages, he outlines the primary ways couples give and receive love. What feels like love to one person may not resonate the same way with another. Understanding both your own and your spouse's love languages is a game changer, allowing you to express affection in a way that truly speaks to them.

The 5 Love languages are:

1. Words of affirmation

2. Acts of service

3. Receiving gifts

4. Quality time

5. Physical touch

Words of affirmation are so vital. They have the power to uplift, build confidence, and nurture the emotional connection.

> *A wife once told her husband,*
> *"You never tell me you love me."*
> *He replied, "Remember, I told you I loved*
> *you on our wedding day."*
> *She nodded, "Yes, I do."*
> *He then added, "Well, if anything changes,*
> *I'll let you know."*

This humorous exchange highlights a common misconception: love, like any important feeling, needs regular expression. Just because it was said once doesn't mean it doesn't need to be reaffirmed. Love grows through consistent reminders, and words of affirmation keep that connection alive.

If I had to prioritize the five love languages, I would say that quality time and physical touch are crucial for both spouses. However, from my observations, men tend to value acts of service more, while women often prioritize words of affirmation. Of course, these are just my personal insights based on my experiences.

At the core, women generally need to feel loved and cherished, while this need isn't as pronounced for men. On the other hand, men crave respect, and that plays a central role in how they connect emotionally.

Providing your spouse with a daily dose of attention, affection, appreciation, and awareness can transform your relationship from good to great, to awesome. What could be easier than remembering the 4 A's as a guiding principle in your daily interactions?

Before we delve into these, it's essential to establish some fundamental rules of civility that every couple should uphold:

Never mock each other.

Always express gratitude to your spouse by saying "please" and "thank you."

These simple practices lay the groundwork for a respectful and loving partnership. Married couples should never belittle, mock, or make jokes at each other's expense. This applies not only to one another, but also to in-laws and family members—be mindful of the jokes you make. If you feel the urge to poke fun, direct it at yourself instead.

In the early stages of a relationship, gestures like opening the car door for your wife or surprising your husband with coffee are common. However, as time goes on, these acts of kindness can fade, leading to a shift from civility to disrespect. It's worth considering recording your conversations and listening to them later; you might be surprised by how differently you communicate with your spouse compared to your friends and neighbors. Would you be rude or dismissive to your partner if it were your first date? If you would not do it on the first date, you should not do it on the 10,000th date.

Attention

Why do so many people keep multiple web pages open while working online? Because it is all about instant access. You should have this same mindset when it comes to your spouse. Make yourself available to them as easily as a web page, so you can respond promptly to their needs. This way they know you are always there for them.

Have you ever found yourself half-listening to your spouse while distracted by your phone, responding with "Uh-huh" as you scroll? Consider how that makes them feel. Think about your own experiences when you're speaking to someone who keeps glancing at their device—it's frustrating and dismissive. Your phone can create a barrier that diminishes the quality of attention you give to those around you, but your spouse is not just anyone. They deserve your full focus and should be the most important person in the room, or out of the room. To cultivate a deeper connection, make it a habit to put your phone away as you get home. This simple act ensures you won't be tempted to answer a text or take a call, allowing you to engage fully with your spouse. This act will show them just how much they matter.

Another effective way to maintain your focus on your spouse is to eliminate the television from your bedroom. Your bedroom should be a serene oasis for just the two of you, free from distractions that can divert your attention away from one another. Having a TV in the room subtly conveys that there are more important activities than spending quality time together. By removing this distraction, you create an environment that encourages intimacy and connection.

Our family dedicates one day each week to disconnect from technology and work, allowing us to connect with one another, without distractions. We put away our phones and computers, and put aside any job-related activities. This day has become our family's favorite, providing us with the opportunity to focus on each other. This practice aligns with the Jewish tradition of Shabbat, a day of rest that many believe contributes to the notably low divorce rates among observant Jews compared to the national average. There's a well-known saying that holds true:

"Families that pray together, stay together." This probably rings true for many religions. This is likely because religion is a shared meaningful purpose that transcends the physical.

If one spouse feels they are not getting enough attention, it's worth reflecting on whether this was an issue prior to marriage. It's unlikely that you would have gotten married if there were signs of neglect back then. So, what has changed? During the dating phase, the primary goal was to gain a deeper connection. This is what makes dating so exhilarating; everything feels fresh and new. You were genuinely interested in getting to know each other, investing time and attention to explore your partner's world. Now that the initial excitement of the relationship has faded, how can you be attentive to your spouse's needs?

The issue may stem from a lack of understanding about what your spouse needs from you. If you don't know what to give to them, you may ignore them and then it's easy to fall into the trap of neglect.

Your fiancé most likely did not hand you a list of their emotional and physical needs before you tied the knot. Instead, you probably made assumptions about what those needs would be. Some couples just make the assumption that what *they* would like in their relationship is the same thing as what their spouse wants. This is a common mistake.

Let's explore this concept further. Understanding your spouse's needs allows you to better navigate how to meet those needs. When you gain this insight, you equip yourself with the tools to strengthen your relationship.

Attention:

The Needs of the Man

Men and women often have different needs when it comes to connection. For instance, when a man returns home from work or a long day, he may seek relaxation and quiet rather than engaging in conversation. This can lead to misunderstandings, as women typically crave more verbal interaction and emotional sharing. While men certainly need attention, it often manifests differently than it does for women. Recognizing these differences is essential for meeting each other's needs effectively.

Some men may come home and head straight for the refrigerator to grab a beer, then settle into their recliner to watch soccer highlights on ESPN. Others might greet their family, but then retreat to the bedroom or bathroom for some alone time. These behaviors can be their way of unwinding, but it's important for partners to understand this need for downtime.

My father had a routine he cherished: every day around 6pm, after he came home from work, he would head to the garden to spend an hour watering, weeding, and picking vegetables. After that, he'd settle in for a nap on the floor next to his bed, asking me or one of my siblings to wake him up when dinner was ready. He found joy in these solitary activities, preferring to recharge in his own way rather than engage in conversation after a long day out. Only after that would he engage with my mother.

When it comes down to the needs of men, they are very simple. There are 3 things that they need in a healthy relationship, food, sex, and respect. Everything else is really a bonus. Men need respect, even more than they desire attention. Whereas women need attention, much more than they desire respect.

They both have a desire for respect *and* attention. It's just that for men, respect from their wife is what they need to feel. For women, love and attention from their husband is more important.

Here's a powerful tip that can help husbands feel respected by their wives. If you take away only one concept from this book, let it be this one; it could truly be a game changer.

When the husband arrives home from work, his wife should be in the middle of a phone conversation loud enough for him to overhear. She should then say, "Sarah, I'll have to call you back; my husband just walked in." She should then hang up the phone and then promptly greet him with "Hi Honey!"

This simple act can transform the atmosphere of the home and truly uplift the husband's spirits. When he walks in and hears his wife stopping what she enjoys doing, just so she can recognize that her husband walks in, makes him feel tremendously appreciated. This works better than if the wife goes running up to her husband, hugging and kissing him and telling him how much she misses and loves him. Which, by the way, rarely happens after a few years of marriage, if ever. Instead of carrying any negative feelings from a tough day, he instantly feels respected and cherished, making him feel like the king of the house.

What's even better is if the wife just pretends to talk on the phone. Even though it is a complete farce, as long as the husband feels respected, it will do wonders for his self-esteem.

If a husband tries this trick on his wife, it likely won't have the same effect on her as it does on him. However, women should definitely give it a try to experience the impact it has and to understand the importance of making men feel respected. I know it works because I love when my wife does it, and I know that many times when she does it, she *is* just pretending. I don't care! It shows me that she respects me, and I love it!

Attention:

The Needs of a Woman

If you've ever watched the NBA playoffs, you may have noticed two women sitting together in prime seats—usually a few rows up from the floor at center court, some of the most expensive seats in the arena. When the camera pans over to them, what are they often doing? Talking. Even if it's Game 7 of a tight series with a trip to the finals on the line! This always leaves me wondering: why spend so much on tickets just to chat through the game? When I go with a buddy, we might exchange only a few words, cheer, have a beer and some peanuts, and still have an incredible time. It highlights a key difference: men generally don't need continuous emotional connection in shared experiences, while for many women, that connection is essential.

Now that we understand that for a husband to feel respect is paramount, the next step is for him to give his wife the attention she craves. When a husband walks into the house for the first time after being apart from his wife for several hours, he needs to ask her these three questions:

- What did you do today?
- What's on your mind?
- How are you feeling?

I know this is hard for men; we just discussed how some men don't really want to talk when they get home. This is a challenge that we men must face—and hopefully overcome—every day of our lives. For those who have a misguided perception that men and women are exactly the same and have the same exact needs, just imagine a wife asking her husband these questions and you will see that it seems ridiculous.

You picked up this book because you're committed to reaching the highest phase of love, so it's up to you if you want to have the best chance of getting there. Many men would rather go mow the lawn than ask your wife these questions. Some would even rather have a colonoscopy. Trust me, I get it—it's a challenge I face myself, and I don't ask these questions every day, just now and then. If your wife knows that you occasionally ask these questions, or if she knows you even *thought* about asking these questions, it can bring a refreshing spark to your marriage.

When you ask your wife these questions, you're bound to notice a shift in your marriage. If she responds to the third question with a curt "Fine!", she's not fine! Take it as a cue that something is bothering her. Don't stop there—dig deeper. Keep asking thoughtful questions to uncover the root of her feelings. Women often need their husbands to listen and provide support, rather than just having all the answers. For the first question, if you know she had a specific event that day, such as a doctor's appointment or a school meeting, reference it directly. This demonstrates that you're engaged with her life and attentive to her needs, which strengthens your emotional connection.

Three Aspects
of Connecting with Your Spouse

The first question, "What did you do today?", focuses on her daily activities and engages her physical side—her hands, legs, and body. Asking this question lets her know you care what her life is like when you aren't with her.

The second question, "What's on your mind?", addresses her thoughts. This demonstrates your genuine interest and encourages her to share what's preoccupying her mind. It affirms that you value her opinions.

The third question, "How are you feeling?", taps into her emotional needs. This is where she truly connects with you—through her heart. By showing genuine interest in her feelings, you create a safe space for her to express herself.

The husband must sit there and listen— for at least 15 seconds. Joking aside, a man has to start somewhere! Even though it may be hard for a man to sit there and listen for too long, with practice, he will start to stay focused for longer and longer periods. Eventually with enough time, he will turn into a husband that his wife deeply loves and respects.

The purpose behind a husband asking these questions lies in their ability to touch upon three aspects that strengthen your bond: physical, intellectual, and emotional. Women, in particular, flourish through emotional connections, which is cultivated through meaningful conversations. This explains why you might find women on the phone for hours—while men also talk on the phone, they tend to be much shorter conversations. For women, meaningful communication is a way to nurture emotional intimacy, which, in turn, fuels their desire for physical intimacy. All a man has to do is listen to his wife and he will get the passion he desires.

The primary reason couples divorce is infidelity— a physical relationship outside the marriage. While infidelity can arise from various factors, it often stems from a lack of emotional connection. As a husband, it's their responsibility to maintain that emotional bond with their wife, and this is why asking those three questions is so crucial.

By actively seeking to understand her feelings, daily experiences, and thoughts, he can reinforce the emotional
intimacy that forms the foundation of a strong and lasting
relationship.

The three forms of connection we've discussed can be
remembered using the acronym **PIE**, which stands for
Physical, **I**ntellectual, and **E**motional connections. This
makes it easy to recall because, let's be honest, who doesn't
love pie?

Just as pie is made up of different delicious layers, your relationship thrives on these three essential components. By
nurturing each aspect—maintaining physical intimacy,
engaging in thoughtful discussions, and fostering emotional bonds—you create a well-rounded and satisfying
partnership that can withstand the test of time.

Emotional connection tends to hold greater significance
for wives than for husbands, though both partners need it
to some degree. In Talmudic law, which is studied in many
places in the world today, the consequences for a married
man's infidelity are less severe than those for a married
woman, which may seem unjust considering the strides
women have made toward equality. The reasoning behind
this is rooted in the different motivations for infidelity.

Men are often more likely to cheat due to opportunity
rather than a search for emotional fulfillment. In contrast,
when a woman strays, it is often driven by a desire for the
emotional support that her husband may not be providing. This difference is why the consequences are viewed
as more severe for women; they are likely to be more emotionally invested in their affair than a man would be.

While a husband may find it easier to detach emotionally from a brief encounter, a woman's infidelity often
indicates a deeper emotional connection with the other

person, making the repair of her marriage almost impossible. It's important to note that these are generalizations, and each instance of infidelity has its own unique set of circumstances.

This explains why many affairs often develop with office colleagues. When people spend long hours at work, they may inadvertently form emotional attachments to co-workers. Even seemingly innocent interactions, such as hugging someone of the opposite sex, can lead to complications. The more you hug someone, the more your feelings grow for them. Although many might not see this as an issue, it likely should be, as the casual acceptance of friendly hugs has, in some cases, led to the breakdown of marriages. This is because hugging triggers the release of oxytocin, a hormone that fosters feelings of bonding and attachment. This can even occur with people who you might not consider attractive. This is why one should place boundaries in professional relationships to protect ones marriage.

While most people acknowledge that physical infidelity is harmful, emotional infidelity can be equally damaging. Forming an emotional bond with someone outside the marriage can undermine the trust and intimacy within the relationship, often setting the stage for potential adultery.

Gary Nueman, author of a book called *Emotional Infidelity,* says the attention we pay to anyone should be mainly to our spouse.[4] Marriage is about relating to a member of the opposite sex with intimacy that is experienced with no other. When a spouse places his or her primary emotional needs in the hands of someone outside the marriage, it breaks the bond of marriage, just as adultery does.

4   Harmony/Rodale Press

Nueman states that if you're married, it's best to avoid friendships with people of the opposite sex. He says:

If you find yourself quick to dismiss my recommendation because it's "ridiculous," "unrealistic," or any other pejorative, ask yourself whether you're being defensive. Challenge yourself to pinpoint the reasons you find my advice so irritating. Could you be avoiding a deeper commitment to your spouse and looking for reasons to seek connection elsewhere?

He continues:

When you get a ping of excitement from an emotionally stimulating moment with someone of the opposite sex (that's not your spouse), you're just chipping away at your marriage. It's dangerous to your marriage, and not just because it may lead to intimacy. It drains your marriage of the immense energy it needs to grow: the energy to flirt with each other, to be emotionally stimulated by a different point of view, to share the excitement with someone who wants to know who you are. When you place your emotional energies elsewhere, without even realizing it, you don't offer your spouse the opportunity to provide you with that same ping of excitement you are looking for elsewhere.

This is precisely why it's crucial for men to maintain an emotional connection with their wives. By asking these three key questions, husbands can create the intimacy that wives deeply crave, strengthening the bond in their marriage.

In real estate investing, the guiding principle for success is often summed up as "Location, location, location." Similarly, if you want to cultivate passion in your marriage, your slogan should be "Attention, attention, attention!"

Affection

Affection is not just a physical action. It encompasses the tone and manner in which you communicate with your spouse. When should you speak to your spouse affectionately? Always. How you talk to them affects how they react to you. Just as children often mirror the behavior of their parents—yelling if they are frequently yelled at or speaking kindly if kindness is modeled—your spouse will respond to the way you address them. Talking to your spouse affectionately is one of the many ways you can get your marriage to the phase of "Never Leaving."

Affection is a fundamental human need, and it should be expressed regularly in your relationship. It doesn't always have to manifest as hugging and kissing; it can be as simple as a gentle brush against your spouse as you walk by in the kitchen or leaning into them when you find yourselves standing close together in an elevator. These subtle gestures can be so discreet that those around you may not even notice, yet they hold profound significance. In fact, these small, everyday acts of affection can strengthen your bond even more than physical intimacy alone, which is of the utmost importance and must occur on a consistent basis.

Be careful about being overly affectionate. Take clues from your spouse and watch their facial expressions and body language; if they appear annoyed, it's because they *are* annoyed.

Many people find it easy to read social cues, but for others, it can be a challenge. If you struggle with this, don't worry—it's a skill you can develop. Enhancing your ability to interpret nonverbal signals is a valuable aspect of practical intelligence that can lead to deeper emotional connections, which we will discuss in Phase 4.

Always communicate with your spouse in an affectionate manner. This means making a conscious effort to avoid raising your voice or resorting to yelling, even in challenging situations. While it may take some practice, the benefits are twofold: not only will it strengthen your marriage, but it will also cultivate a sense of calm within you.

Appreciation

Women thrive on appreciation, and while men may not need it as much, they certainly value it too. If your husband sets the table for dinner, take a moment to express your gratitude. If you don't like the way he does it, don't criticize him! Let him do it the way he wants, then, when he leaves the room, fix the table the way you like it.

If he goes shopping for the family or lends a hand with any task, make it a point to acknowledge his efforts and reinforce his role as an integral part of your family. Even if he does very little chores in your house, find any small way to show appreciation for him. It's possible that he doesn't contribute more simply because he hasn't received positive feedback in the past.

People often rise to the expectations set for them. When you label someone negatively—like calling them lazy—they may internalize that label, making it a self-fulfilling prophecy. The power of suggestion is incredibly potent. By offering your husband genuine appreciation, you can shift his mindset and potentially inspire him to engage more actively in helping around the house. Your acknowledgment could be the catalyst for positive change in your relationship.

For men, it's essential to express gratitude when your wife cooks dinner, regardless of the outcome. Even if the meat turns out burnt, find something positive to highlight—perhaps the flavor of the seasoning or the effort she put into the meal. A simple acknowledgment of her efforts can make a world of difference and encourage her to continue putting her heart into the meals she prepares for you. Remember, appreciation is a vital part of nurturing your relationship.

Men need to pay attention and complement their wife's appearance. Women care a great deal about what they wear—everything from the scarf on their head down to the shoes on their feet. Every piece is an important part of their ensemble. Have you ever heard your wife say she has nothing to wear? Forget the fact that she has ten times the closet space as you, and it is completely filled with shoes and clothes. If you're bothered by how much money your wife spends on clothes, occasionally compliment her on what she's wearing. If you don't, she may keep on buying clothes until you recognize how good she looks!

Whenever your wife buys a new pair of shoes, a dress, or a scarf and asks for your opinion, always respond by telling her she looks beautiful. Consistently showing your spouse appreciation is essential, regardless of how she appears on any given day. For extra points, refer to an outfit she previously wore to a special event and express how much you loved it: "Honey, do you remember that stunning red dress you wore to my nephew's wedding? I'd love to see you wear that again!" This not only shows that you notice her, but also reignites her passion for you. Nothing brings a woman more joy than knowing that her husband remembers and cherishes what she wore months ago!

Awareness

When I wrote my first marriage book, I didn't initially include the idea of awareness. It was my wife who encouraged me to add it, pointing out that I sometimes failed to notice where she was, even in simple situations. For instance, while we would walk down the street as a family, I'd get caught up in conversation with one of our children and lose track of her. This lack of awareness extended beyond that moment, but it highlighted an important lesson: always be aware of where your spouse is at any given time. By doing so, you reinforce the feeling that they are always on your mind.

Being aware of each other's needs is crucial in a marriage. For instance, my wife occasionally texts me when she's running low on something, and I make it a point to get it for her. I know she appreciates this little gesture. Similarly, I feel a genuine sense of happiness when she picks up on my casual complaints—like my shortage of socks—and surprises me with a new bag of socks from Amazon. It's these thoughtful actions that show we're truly listening to one another and willing to go the extra mile to meet each other's needs, fostering a deeper connection between us.

There is an issue in marriages that seems to be overlooked and can be a major issue. I understand that men need to do a better job of listening, but women should also have the awareness that men have a limited capacity for listening. Since listening is such an important part of a healthy marriage, it should be something that people work on early on, even as early as the Crush Phase.

Case Study: *During a visit to Chicago, a middle-aged woman approached me after one of my classes seeking advice. She shared that her husband sometimes walks out of the room while she's in the middle of talking to him. I told her I could relate because I've done something similar myself.*

I recalled a time when I came home from work, and my wife was telling me about her day. In the middle of her story,

I suddenly remembered that there were chocolate glazed doughnuts in the kitchen. Without thinking, I walked away to grab one. My wife called me out, asking if I had just walked out on her mid-conversation. I apologized and explained what had happened, but it was clear that I hurt her feelings.

I shared this story with the woman and suggested that her husband might need to work on being more present while listening. At the same time, I advised her to consider her husband's listening capacity— it's not unlimited. A helpful approach might be to communicate in bullet points, making it easier for him to stay engaged in the conversation.

While men should work on becoming better listeners, women can benefit from understanding that men often have limited listening bandwidth. Recognizing this dynamic can foster more positive and effective communication in the marriage.

Focus on the four A's: Attention, Affection, Appreciation, and Awareness. Keep these words at the forefront of your mind. The more you remind yourself to embody these principles, the more naturally they will integrate into your daily interactions. This intentional practice will not only enhance the passion in your relationship, but also significantly increase your chances of achieving that elusive state of "Never Leaving."

A Monthly Honeymoon

D o you still feel the same spark with your spouse that you did early in your marriage? Regardless of your answer, there's always room to deepen that connection. You may have heard of the "seven-year itch." Thankfully, it's not a skin condition (and if it were, you'd definitely want to avoid it!). Instead, it's the term for the point in a relationship—often around seven years—when one or both partners might feel the excitement has waned. This can lead some to seek new relationships rather than reigniting the passion in their current marriage.

That same feeling you had in the beginning is often still there—it just needs to be rekindled.

How do you make your relationship feel fresh and exciting again? How do you bring back that spark and passion you felt when you first met or got married? Let's dive into some key ideas that can help you keep the passion alive.

Exercise

Strenuous exercise can increase the passion in all your relationships. Sure, a little soreness might come with it, but that's nothing compared to the pain of getting a divorce! Any activity that gets your heart pumping is fantastic, though running is the most efficient and has the greatest impact. While many people seek youth through vitamins or plastic surgery, the true, lasting benefits often come from regular, vigorous exercise.

In today's world, most of us live sedentary lives. We no longer trek to the river to fetch water or hunt for our meals. Instead, almost everything we need is just a tap or a click away, requiring little effort. But this lack of movement can take a toll on our mood, energy, and ultimately, the way we connect with our loved ones. Regular exercise isn't just about fitness; it's essential for mental well-being.

Exercise naturally boosts serotonin, sometimes called the "happy chemical," in our brains. As we age, our serotonin production declines, which can lead to depression, anxiety, and sleep problems. The good news is that regular exercise can help counter this by elevating serotonin levels, improving your mood and overall sense of well-being. With more energy and patience, you'll bring renewed passion to your relationship.

In colleges worldwide, students often experiment with various drugs in search of a good feeling. Consistent running offers what I like to call "free drugs"—no cost or harmful side effects, and a natural high. The benefits include improved health and a whole range of other positive effects.

To be clear, while a leisurely three-mile walk is beneficial, it won't generate the serotonin boost needed to shift your outlook on life. For that, you need exercise that significantly raises your heart rate—making you sweat and breathe hard. Sitting on a stationary bike and lightly pedaling while reading a book won't cut it! Although yoga is fantastic for health and flexibility, most yoga classes aren't strenuous enough to trigger that serotonin surge. Choose an activity that pushes you physically, as that's what will have the greatest positive impact on your relationships.

Getting Motivated to Start Exercising

You're not going to meet your future spouse or improve your current marriage while sitting on the couch eating bonbons. You have to get off your tush and get started. That's exactly the mindset I had to adopt when I decided to get back in shape.

Back in college, I worked at a pizza shop, making pizzas from scratch every day. For every slice I sold, I'd eat one. Twenty-five pounds later, I left college overweight.

I was unhappy with my appearance and low stamina, so I decided to start running. At first, I could barely run a single block before feeling winded, but I got up and ran that one short block—it only took a few minutes, but it was a start. Each day, I aimed to add another 20 or 30 feet, just making it to the next driveway. Little by little, I built momentum.

After a couple of weeks, I managed to run four blocks, and before long, I could run a full mile! That was a big milestone because once I could run one mile, two miles was within reach. And once I hit two miles, running a 5k or even a 10k started to feel possible.

At this point, you can confidently call yourself a runner, and the feeling is amazing! The positive changes in your life become evident as you experience a surge of happiness and energy. The exhilaration of a runner's high is where your body and soul are at peace in perfect harmony. This newfound vitality translates into greater passion and stamina for everything you pursue, especially for cultivating a thriving relationship.

> *"The exhilaration of a runner's high is where your body and soul are at peace in perfect harmony."*

Incorporating just a bit of exercise into your daily routine can lead to significant improvements over time, even if it's as simple as running a few blocks. If the idea of running feels daunting, consider breaking it down into manageable chunks. For example, running a quarter mile four times throughout the day is just as effective as completing a mile in one go. To inspire you to take those small steps toward the transformation you desire, here is a helpful analogy:

> *"A NASA rocket scientist is sending a satellite to a planet in a galaxy far, far away. Unbeknownst to him, the direction the rocket is headed is off by about one centimeter. No one notices the error until well after the rocket has left Earth's atmosphere and entered outer space. What seems like just a tiny error, can end up sending the satellite to a completely wrong galaxy, millions of miles from its intended destination."*

If it only takes a tiny error to throw the rocket off course by millions of miles, then making just a small correction earlier would have put the rocket back on track to reach its destination.

If your life is off course, it can significantly impact your relationships. Just one small change today can have a tremendous impact months or years down the road. This analogy applies to every aspect of life. Just start small, and eventually all those small changes in your life will put you back on course to enhance the relationship you currently have.

There is no excuse for you not to run to the end of the block and back. Go run, *now!*

Get Rid of the Uncertainty

I like to refer to an issue I call sexual ambiguity. Sexual ambiguity arises when one spouse is eager for intimacy while the other isn't interested. For example, he's ready to go, but she's feeling a bit under the weather, or she longs for closeness while he's too drained from work.

As marriages evolve, the likelihood of encountering uncertainty grows. This uncertainty can introduce stress into the relationship, often compounding over time and potentially leading to its breakdown. A strong physical bond is essential for a healthy marriage, and when ambiguity arises in this area, it can become a slippery slope, increasing the risk of infidelity or divorce.

There's also the risk of monotony, which can creep in when you're with the same spouse for a lifetime. So, how can both of you maintain the physicality and passion that characterized the early days of your marriage?

You've likely heard of the concept of "date night," a valuable tool for married couples to reconnect, especially those with children. Amid the daily hustle and bustle, it's easy to lose sight of why you fell in love in the first place. Setting aside dedicated time for just the two of you allows for meaningful rekindling of your bond. Prioritizing time together without the kids is crucial; it creates space for intimacy that often gets overshadowed by family responsibilities.

While date night may help address the issue of this uncertainty in a marriage, it's not a guaranteed solution. So, how can you effectively tackle this challenge that many couples face? Is there a way to eliminate sexual ambiguity so when you go to bed you are clear on whether you will be physical together?

Fire and Water Don't Mix

Every couple yearns for two essential elements in their relationship: a fire-like intensity and a water-like calmness. What sets fire and water apart? Fire is hot, passionate, and electrifying. It symbolizes a relationship filled with desire, excitement, and fervent love—the exhilarating feelings that many couples recall experiencing early in their marriage. The challenge, however, lies in sustaining that fiery passion over time. We want to feel that rush when our spouse enters the room, a yearning to be close, to ignite our passion, and to connect as if we are two souls merging into one.

On the other hand, water embodies a relationship that is dependable, calm, tranquil, and consistent—much like a gentle stream, its soothing sounds flowing over smooth rocks. This stability is essential in a marriage, as a relationship can't thrive solely on fiery passion. We also need moments of serenity, where we can simply be ourselves. While a relationship grounded in water may function for a time, your spouse may become almost like a loyal business partner. They are always there when you need them, but you eventually miss the fire.

Here's where the challenge lies for most couples. Fire and water can't survive together. No scientist has successfully combined the two; either the fire evaporates the water, or the water extinguishes the fire. So how can you nurture both a both a fiery relationship and a water-like relationship?

Keeping it Fresh

We can gain valuable insights about marriage from the Jewish tradition, which has been preserved for thousands of years. You don't need to be Jewish or adhere to any particular faith to appreciate these teachings. If something has endured for millennia, it likely holds significant wisdom. Among these traditions are the laws of family purity.

When a woman experiences her monthly cycle, the couple typically separates for about two weeks. During this time, they refrain from hugging, kissing, or possibly even sharing the same bed. This intentional break from physical intimacy allows for a significant shift in their relationship dynamic. With the physical aspect temporarily set aside, the emotional connection takes center stage, fostering deeper conversations, and understanding, on a more profound level.

As the two-week period draws to a close, an exhilarating sense of anticipation begins to build. This heightened desire can manifest romantically, creating electricity between the spouses. The thrilling tension draws them closer together, igniting the spark of passion and intimacy that they have been longing for.

Just like anything else in life, when something is constantly available, it tends to lose its allure. The excitement and special feelings you once had with your spouse when you first got married can fade over time. The thrill of anticipation diminishes, making those once-sparkling moments feel more routine and less extraordinary.

When the break finally concludes, the woman immerses herself in a spiritual bath known as a Mikvah, and then it's time for the fireworks! It's just like being on their honeymoon. The desire to be passionately together returns, just as when they were first together.

Taking a physical break, even for a short period, can be a powerful step toward reigniting the passion in your marriage. Start with a few days and gradually extend the duration each month until you discover the optimal time that helps recreate that exhilarating feeling of being together for the first time. This approach can effectively eliminate the dilemma of sexual ambiguity. A couple is either on or off. This removes any ambiguity about physical intimacy, which will significantly reduce stress in your relationship.

After her cycle, a woman typically makes herself available to her husband without excuses like "I have a headache" or "I'm too tired." During the off period, there's no room for last-minute disappointments or uncertainty; the husband can then arrange his evenings without worry that he won't be needed for intimacy with his wife. He can then spend time with friends or attend sporting events stress free. Knowing this takes so much stress off of the relationship.

While introducing a physical break in your marriage may feel challenging, the effort can lead to a deeply passionate relationship as a reward. It's relatively easy to find a partner and reach the commitment stage, but navigating the journey to the phase of "Never Leaving" is far more complex. Just as running is one of the most efficient forms of exercise, intentionally taking a break from physical intimacy might also be the catalyst for rekindling the passion in your relationship.

Infinite Marriage

The Infinite Marriage represents a marriage that is nurtured, developed, and sustained not only for your lifetime, but also for your children and future generations. If you want your children to experience a great marriage, you must model what a great marriage looks like. It all begins with you! The effort you invest in your marriage isn't just a one-time commitment; it's a continuous journey. Every action you take to foster a strong relationship today lays the groundwork for a legacy that extends far beyond your lifetime. This perspective is essential for building anything that thrives in the long run.

"...if you want your children to experience a great marriage, you must model what a great marriage looks like."

In Simon Sinek's bestselling book, The Infinite Game, he explores how adopting a finite mindset in business can hinder long-term success.[5] When leaders focus solely on achieving immediate goals, they risk overlooking the sustainability of their organizations. Many executives prioritize short-term financial gains or sales targets, often influenced by their compensation packages, which can misalign their goals with investors. In contrast, an infinite mindset encourages leaders to think about the company's future—what it will look like in 20, 30 years, and beyond. This approach ultimately leads to a more sustainable and successful business.

Amazon exemplifies the power of an infinite mindset. For years, the company operated at a loss, leading many investors to question its viability. Yet, under the leadership of founder and CEO Jeff Bezos, the focus remained steadfastly on long-term growth and innovation. Bezos prioritized building a sustainable business model over appeasing short-term traders or immediate financial returns. His vision was not just about the next quarter, but about where Amazon would be in 20 years and beyond. This commitment to the future has ultimately positioned Amazon as one of the most valuable companies of all time, demonstrating that patience and a long-term perspective can yield extraordinary results.

This same mindset should be applied to your marriage. Creating an Infinite Marriage can actually be more straightforward than establishing a long-lasting business. Unlike businesses that often grapple with financial constraints and the constant need for funding, a thriving marriage doesn't always have to contend with such pressures. Instead of worrying running out of money, the primary concern in a marriage is running out of patience. While businesses focus on immediate profitability, your relationship can flourish with the right investment of time, effort, and love, ensuring its longevity for future generations.

What constitutes a finite marriage? A marriage based on a specific physical goal. Earlier in this book, we explored the idea of marrying primarily for reasons such as having children or other physical aspects of the relationship. While children can indeed be a compelling reason to marry, they shouldn't be the sole focus. A successful marriage requires a deeper foundation that extends beyond the physical. As you enter the Commitment Phase, it's essential to start contemplating the long-term vision of your relationship. Considering what lies beyond your lifetime may not be at the forefront of your thoughts when dating, but this perspective is crucial as you solidify your commitment to one another.

How can you ground your marriage in the Infinite Marriage? What steps can you do to lay a solid foundation for your entire life together—and ideally for your children's children?

Here are ten key strategies to help you get started. Just as Steve Jobs built Apple and Warren Buffet grew Berkshire Hathaway, you too are laying the groundwork for a legacy that can span generations.

1. **Never raise your voice**—I know this can be challenging for some, but with practice, it's entirely achievable. Different strategies work for different people: some count to ten when anger strikes, others bite their tongues, while some retreat to another room and beat up a pillow. Recognizing that yelling rarely accomplishes anything, except fulfilling your desire to get angry. Often, those who tend to show their anger

have learned this behavior from their parents. If you find yourself struggling to keep your voice down, try to pause and transition to a calm tone as soon as you can. If you can't, leave the room and go somewhere else where you can vent without anyone hearing or seeing you; and then you can beat up a pillow if you need to.

2. **Be resilient**—Resilience is one of the most valuable traits to have in a spouse. Resilient individuals remain calm and collected in the face of adversity. They don't complain about dirty hotels. Instead they say they that they are happy that they don't have to sleep on a park bench. They don't complain about airline food. Instead, they comment how amazing it is they are sitting in an aluminum tub, flying 600 miles-per-hour at 40,000 feet above the earth while the flight attendant is pouring them a 7-Up and giving them a hot meal. If they encounter a dirty glass at a restaurant, they simply take a napkin and wipe it down instead of making a fuss. They don't panic and go to the hospital when their child has a fever or hits their head on the corner of a table. They wait calmly and use ice or a cold bath to reduce the fever or swelling. They don't panic about the current diseases being plastered all over the media. They think for themselves and take precautions that make sense.

3. **Be vulnerable**—Embracing vulnerability allows your authentic emotions to surface and is a hallmark of emotional health. We can learn a lot about being vulnerable from a lobster. A lobster is a soft, mushy animal that lives underwater in a hard shell. When its body grows, it becomes very uncomfortable because its shell does not grow with it. To adapt, the lobster undergoes a molting process, shedding its old shell.

In this moment of transition, it becomes highly vulnerable, lacking protection from predators. To protect itself, it hides beneath rocks or reefs until its new shell hardens.

Just like the lobster, being vulnerable in your marriage requires courage. It means opening up about your fears, insecurities, and feelings without the immediate safety of your emotional "shell." By allowing yourself to be vulnerable, you create deeper intimacy and trust with your spouse.

When we feel uncomfortable or are in emotional pain, what do we do? What many of us don't do is figuratively "lose our shell" and allow ourselves to be vulnerable and grow. Instead, we go see a doctor, who may prescribe anti-anxiety medication. These drugs numb our feelings, but this approach can create a cycle of avoidance, preventing us from facing and processing our emotions, ultimately hindering our connection in relationships. True healing and growth come from confronting our discomfort and allowing ourselves to be open and vulnerable.

You can't be authentic when you're focused on pleasing others, pretending to be someone you're not, or suppressing your true feelings. Bottling up emotions will inevitably lead to emotional turmoil, creating a finite relationship that lacks depth. In contrast, an infinite marriage thrives on vulnerability. It involves acknowledging your insecurities and anxieties and confronting them head-on. This honest self-examination can be challenging, but it's essential for building genuine emotional intimacy with your spouse.

No one enjoys being vulnerable; it's inherently challenging. Admitting "I'm wrong" can feel like a defeat,

saying "I love you" opens up your heart, and expressing "I need help" requires humility. Yet, personal
growth hinges on your ability to embrace vulnerability, particularly in your marriage. This willingness to
share your true self—flaws, fears, and all—creates an
environment of trust and intimacy. It's through these
authentic exchanges that you can become the person
you're truly meant to be, both for yourself and your
spouse. Vulnerability may be uncomfortable, but it's
a crucial step toward deeper connections and a more
fulfilling relationship.

4. **Judge everyone favorably**—It is very easy to find
    fault with people and always focus on their negative
    characteristics, even if you only do it with people you
    don't know well. Someone who is working on an in-
    finite marriage will focus on the positive aspects of
    everyone they meet, *especially* those they don't know.
    If you can judge people favorably that you don't know,
    think about how much easier it will be to judge the
    closest person in your life favorably; your spouse!

    One effective approach to foster understanding and
    empathy is to view each new person you meet as
    a 50-chapter book. When you encounter someone—
    especially in a negative context—you're only witness-
    ing a single chapter of their story. They might be in
    Chapter 25, and you have no insight into the first
    24 chapters that shaped who they are today. Perhaps
    they've experienced emotional trauma or faced chal-
    lenges you know nothing about. Keeping this per-
    spective in mind can help temper your reactions and
    judgments. After all, you have no idea what the final
    chapters of their book will reveal. Their story may
    culminate in a beautiful, uplifting conclusion!

5. **Speak positively**—Creating an Infinite Marriage begins with a culture of positive communication. This means refraining from criticizing your spouse and instead using language that uplifts and encourages. Just as negative speech can undermine and tear someone down, positive words have the power to build them up. By consciously choosing to focus on the positive aspects of your relationship and expressing appreciation, you can shift your mode of communication.

6. **Embrace life**—Celebrate the beauty in everyday moments, whether it's a rainy day or muddy floors. Open your doors and windows to let in fresh air, welcoming the world outside. Don't fret over the occasional bug that might wander in; instead, embrace your resilience and remember that a little chaos can add character to life. By choosing to find joy in these imperfect moments, you cultivate a spirit of appreciation and adventure that can invigorate your relationship and create lasting memories together.

7. **Never quit**—Always demonstrate that you are not a quitter. It's perfectly acceptable to step away from a situation to gain clarity, but make sure you return with renewed determination to keep trying. Approach challenges with creativity and an open mind, looking for solutions outside the norm. Remember, when you give up, you're choosing a finite mindset. Instead, embrace the infinite—persevere, adapt, and keep pushing forward, even when the going gets tough!

8. **Don't take things personally**—Remember, no one is out to get you! When your spouse acts in a way that feels insulting, resist the urge to take it to heart. Often, their actions are not meant to be personal; they may stem from their own insecurities or the influence of a difficult upbringing. Finite relationships often

suffer when partners interpret each other's behavior as a personal attack. In contrast, infinite relationships thrive on the understanding that your spouse genuinely wants the best for you and would never deliberately cause you pain. Cultivate this mindset, and you'll find it much easier to navigate challenges together.

The most effective way to alleviate the stress of interacting with a difficult person is to cultivate compassion for them and offer assistance when you can. Often, those who behave inappropriately are carrying far more emotional baggage than you might realize. Take a moment to be grateful that you aren't facing the same struggles they are. Remember, people can evolve and transform into remarkable individuals over time. While you can't change someone else, you can change your reaction to them. By responding with understanding and kindness, you create an environment that may inspire positive change in them.

9. **Try to see someone else's perspective**—Strive to understand situations from your spouse's point of view. Your perception of the world is shaped by your unique experiences, just as theirs is shaped by theirs. For instance, if you grew up in a chaotic household while your spouse was raised in a calm and organized environment, your backgrounds create differing realities. These differences can lead to misunderstandings, prompting one spouse to exclaim, "Why can't you just be like me?" The truth is, they can't—because they are not you. Recognize that each person has their own way of doing things, and that doesn't make either of you wrong. Instead of adopting a judgmental attitude, embrace a mindset of appreciation. Aim to complement each other's differences rather than criticize them.

10. **Consider the Impact of Your Actions on Others—**
At the heart of the Infinite Marriage is the awareness of how your actions ripple out to affect those around you, and potentially future generations. If your behavior could harm others—whether through fighting, yelling, lying, arguing, cheating, acting irresponsibly, or being overly critical—it's worth reconsidering those actions. Reflect on how your choices resonate beyond the immediate moment, shaping not only your relationship, but also setting a precedent for future generations.

When Divorce
is Necessary

Although marriage can be hard if you don't have the proper tools, I have been told that divorce will be even worse. Divorce is often compared to death. This is why not discussing divorce in a book about love would be just sweeping it under the proverbial rug. The idea that if we don't talk about it, then it doesn't exist, is not something that will instill clarity in your life.

One of the reasons I decided to write this book is that I discovered that it is hard to sell, or even give away, a book on marriage. Those in a thriving marriage feel that they have no need to read a book about something that they don't need help with. For those that are struggling with their marriage, the prospect of reading solutions may be too painful. Everyone wants to be in love and if you have a clearer understanding of what love is, you'll have a better shot at a great marriage. This is why I decided to combine love, dating and marriage into one book.

The risk of divorce begins the moment you say "I do." This reality should inspire you to seek knowledge about how to be in a healthy relationship before challenges arise. Many divorces could have been prevented if couples had embraced even a few of the concepts discussed in this book early in their marriage.

John Gottman, a prominent marriage researcher, asserts that he can predict divorce with an impressive 94% accuracy. In his lab, he observes married couples' vital signs while identifying a flashpoint that triggers disagreement. What he specifically looks for is a damaging emotion known as "contempt." This occurs when one spouse not only disagrees, but also disrespects the other's viewpoint, manifesting as eye-rolling or dismissive thoughts that label differing opinions as foolish.

Contempt can be especially potent in marriage, where the emotional investment amplifies the reactions. Unlike differences with acquaintances, which may be shrugged off, contempt erodes the foundation of love and respect essential for a healthy relationship. It's akin to swimming in the ocean without applying sunscreen; over time, the damage accumulates until the relationship is burnt.

In today's throwaway society, marriage has become increasingly viewed as disposable. Divorce is so common that it rarely raises eyebrows; in fact, in some American communities, it's almost expected. This casual approach to relationships can lead to a lack of commitment and a diminished appreciation for the effort required to sustain a marriage. As a result, many couples may overlook the importance of nurturing their bond.

In my view, couples often divorce when the pain of being married outweighs the pleasure. While pain can a natural part of any relationship, one must have a vision of the future pleasure that can result from the work that it will take to improve a marriage. If couples see little hope ahead, it becomes increasingly difficult to navigate the challenges. However, when you can shift your focus to the pleasure of your relationship, it becomes much easier to manage the discomfort that arises.

Is there a significant amount of pain involved in being an Olympic athlete? Absolutely! These athletes dedicate their entire lives to reaching the pinnacle of their sport, sacrificing sleep, education, and leisure time along the way. They endure this pain because they have a clear vision of the incredible rewards that await them as a result of their hard work. The promise of achieving their dreams and the joy of competing at the highest level makes all the sacrifices worthwhile.

Picture a group of boys playing basketball under the scorching summer sun. They can play for hours on end, fueled by the joy of the game. However, remove the ball and ask them to continue, and they wouldn't last five minutes. The reason is simple: they can endure the physical strain because they are immersed in the pleasure of playing. Without the ball, even though they're engaged in the same activity of running up and down the court, the enjoyment evaporates. Suddenly, what was once fun becomes a painful chore, highlighting how pleasure can transform to pain in a split second.

So, how do you know when it's time to consider divorce? It often comes down to recognizing when the pain has become overwhelming, despite your best efforts to repair the relationship. If you've exhausted all avenues for reconciliation and the emotional toll becomes unbearable, it may be a sign that it's time to reevaluate your situation.

Imagine you're in a serious car accident and severely injure your leg. The doctor informs you that there's a 50/50 chance of saving it, but it will require multiple painful

surgeries and years of therapy. However, he can ampu-
tate your leg to spare you from that lengthy ordeal. What
would you choose? Many would choose to go through the
pain in hopes of saving their leg.

This analogy mirrors what it takes to save a marriage. Just
as it can be painful to repair a leg, mending a relationship
often involves navigating a difficult emotional journey.
If you're willing to endure significant pain to preserve
something as vital as a limb, you should also be prepared
to confront even greater pain to save your marriage.

You will only consider amputation when the pain in your
leg becomes unbearable, signaling that the situation is no
longer sustainable. Similarly, in a marriage, it's only when
the emotional pain is so unbearable that you know it's
time to get a divorce.

Divorce is so common today because many individuals
are unwilling to endure the pain necessary to save their
marriage. Viewing marriage as a union of two souls can
shift this perspective; if you see your spouse as part of
you, you're more likely to invest the effort to save your
relationship, just as you would fight to preserve your own
leg. Every marriage will inevitably face challenges and
pain at some point. To avoid divorce, it's crucial to keep
your focus on the pleasure—the love that initially brought
you together. This can provide the motivation to help you
work through the difficult times.

Phase 4

NEVER LEAVING

We're now in the final stage of the 4 Phases of Love—a phase that is challenging for many people to implement, which is why many couples may never reach it. Think of this phase like a critical upgrade for your marriage, similar to updating the operating system on your computer to improve performance. This phase is to marriage what reaching the summit is to Mount Everest. Just as climbing Everest requires months of preparation, money, and time, achieving this phase requires patience and emotional effort. Thankfully, unlike the 14% death rate of Everest climbers, what's at stake here is overcoming the 75% (possibly much more) risk of enduring an unhappy marriage.

This is the place I hope every reader reaches—the point where you can honestly say about your marriage, "I am never leaving."

What's Important to You Is Important to Me

One way to ensure you reach the point of the Never Leaving relationship is by understanding and prioritizing your spouse's needs. This doesn't mean you need to fully understand the "why" behind each need; it simply means recognizing that if it matters to them, it needs to matter to you—even if it seems unimportant or confusing. This mindset is a crucial foundation for lasting intimacy. Often, it's the little gestures—the seemingly trivial acts repeated consistently—that make the biggest impact on a relationship. These small, daily acts of giving yourself to your spouse foster an enduring bond far more than any grand vacation, luxury car, or dream home ever could.

Early in my marriage, I would take my wife to modern dance performances, even though I am not a big fan. Similarly, she would come with me to the symphony, though the music didn't resonate with her the way it does with me, and she often fell asleep. Yet, we both happily went for each other's interests because they mattered to us as a couple. We recognized that part of building a strong marriage is doing things for each other that we might not do on our own. Most couples understand and agree with this principle.

Here's where things get interesting. We have an unwritten rule in our home: I handle all the cooking, and my wife takes care of cleaning up afterward, ideally with some help from the kids. As a bit of a neat freak, I like to keep things tidy as I cook, making sure everything I use ends up in the sink so the counters stay clean—even the sharp kitchen knives.

She asked me a few times, very kindly, if I could leave the sharp knives on the kitchen counter instead of placing them in the sink, as she was concerned about accidentally cutting herself. Her request made perfect sense—it was a simple step to avoid potential injury.

On the other hand, I wanted to ensure the countertop was spotless, which to me meant nothing should be left on it. In my view, if a dirty knife is on the countertop, that countertop wasn't clean. So, despite her reasonable request, I found it difficult to comply—it conflicted with my compulsive need for a spotless kitchen.

Deciding where knives should go might seem like a minor issue in a marriage, and most relationships could easily withstand such a small disagreement. But if you're reading this book, it's because you're aiming for more than just an average marriage. We'll return to this point shortly.

Another small but recurring matter was the size of the fork I would bring my wife at mealtime. When I set the table, I'd grab a handful of small forks from the utensil drawer, since we had young children. I'd also give my wife a small fork along with the rest of us. She would politely ask for a large one instead, and without hesitation, I'd exchange it for her.

Eventually, I realized that my wife truly preferred using a large fork. At first, I didn't give much thought to her preference—fork size didn't matter to me, so I assumed it didn't matter to her either. This was my ego getting in the way of what she had clearly expressed she wanted. After repeatedly handing her a small fork, only to go back and swap it for a large one at her request, it finally sank in that I should just grab her a large fork to begin with.

Seriously, I'll eat with any fork. The size of the fork does not make a difference to me. I'll even eat with a spoon if there is no fork around. Just give me some chopsticks, salad tongs, or even a toothpick. I'll use whatever instrument is available to get food into my mouth as efficiently as possible.

What does the size of a dinner fork and where I put dirty knives matter? The point I want to make is that *it doesn't matter what I think.* If I want my marriage to get to the point of Never Leaving, I must care about what *my wife* thinks!

Marriage is not about me—marriage is about we! I must learn to view things from her perspective, recognizing that what may seem trivial to me could hold significant meaning for her.

After a lot of introspection, I realized that the small fork issue was more significant than I initially thought. I finally made the conscious effort to stop bringing my wife the small fork and to stop leaving the sharp knives in the sink. Was this change difficult? In some ways, yes and in others, no. Training myself to avoid putting the knives in the sink and to offer her the larger fork was pretty easy. The real difficulty lay in understanding why I needed to adjust my behavior and recognizing that these seemingly trivial matters weren't so trivial.

It didn't happen overnight. Change takes time for me, and I had to teach my ego that I'm not the only one in this relationship. With practice, I eventually stopped putting the sharp knives in the sink and learned to always offer my wife a large fork when I bring her dinner. The hardest part for me was overcoming my ego, which had kept me from responding to her needs. Embracing the idea that "what's important to you is important to me" means recognizing that there will be moments when something makes no sense to you, but that doesn't matter. The key is to understand that you're not just living with your own perspective; you're sharing life with someone else, and their viewpoint is just as valid and important as yours.

For my wife and me, this same concept applies to flowers. Why would anyone spend perfectly good money on a dying plant? Because that's what flowers are. Once you pick them, they start the dying process. I understand flowers are pretty and they brighten up a room, the most important factor is that my wife truly loves them. So I trek every week to the florist and spend $20 for flowers for our Shabbat table, and $50 if it's a holiday. I may not personally care much for flowers, but I've learned that if something is important to her, it must also be important to me.

Here's the deeper reason behind our discussion of forks, knives, and flowers, and why it should resonate with you: Every time I leave the kitchen with a large fork, my wife knows that I'm thinking of her. When I clean the kitchen and leave a knife neatly beside the sink instead of in it, she knows I'm thinking of her. Each time I bring home flowers, she knows I'm thinking of her. But what is even more important is that she knows I am doing something that means absolutely nothing to me! This reinforces her love and strengthens our emotional connection. She knows I'm going out of my way to do what makes her happy because she knows that what is important to her, is important to me.

Some men appreciate it when they know their wife is thinking about them, but even more women would cherish the same thing from their husbands. It's not only the grand gestures in life that your spouse cares about; it's the small everyday actions that demonstrate that you care, especially when it is for them. This is a very important concept to understand and embody in order to have a marriage full of bliss. If you don't agree with me, then you definitely need to read the next chapter. Or you can forget the large fork, order sushi, and just eat with your fingers.

Sometimes You Have
to be Wrong
to be Right

There's a well-known saying that goes, "If your wife is happy, you're likely to be happy." While death and taxes are often seen as life's two certainties, the phrase "happy wife, happy life" might just be the third. Unlike death and taxes, which are beyond our control, your wife's happiness is something you can actively influence. So, why not focus on nurturing that happiness? It's the one certainty you have the power to impact, and doing so can lead to a more fulfilling life for both of you.

You might wonder why your wife's happiness is so crucial to a mans happiness. The reality is that many decisions in a marriage hinge on her agreement. For instance, if you're considering moving to a new neighborhood, but your wife isn't on board, chances are, you won't be moving. Similarly, when it comes to choosing the children's school, it's often the wife who takes the lead in making that decision. Even when planning a vacation, if the husband

and wife have different destinations in mind, she's likely to get her way unless he negotiates. This isn't just about compromise; it's rooted in the understanding that your vacation will be far more enjoyable if she's happy with the destination.

I understand that some men may disagree with this perspective. If thats the case, I encourage you to take a moment for self-reflection. Consider why you might struggle to accommodate your wife's desires. Is it your ego getting in the way, or is there another underlying issue at play? It's crucial to recognize that if your motivation for "winning" an argument is simply about being right, your ego may not be your amigo. Such attitudes can have a detrimental impact on your marriage. Instead of allowing pride to obstruct your path, focus on fostering a collaborative relationship that benefits both partners.

I have a personal mantra that I repeat to myself during disagreements with my wife, and while it may seem counterintuitive, it can significantly impact your journey toward reaching the phase of "Never Leaving." The mantra is: "Sometimes you have to be wrong to be right." This means that even when you're convinced you're right, it can be beneficial to set aside your pride and admit you're wrong. Embracing this mindset isn't always easy, but it can truly transform the dynamics of a marriage.

Have you ever found yourself in a heated argument with your spouse, convinced you were right? You might argue for hours, and eventually, they might concede and admit you were correct. But the real question is: did you truly win? While you may have won that battle, you might have lost the war. It's essential to recognize that the need to "win" often isn't worth the emotional toll it takes on your marriage. Instead of clinging to your victory, consider letting go of that urge. Disagreements don't have to escalate into conflicts; sometimes, the best approach is to yield, even if you believe you're in the right. Admitting you were wrong—even occasionally—can foster a sense of understanding that you're better off happy than right.

The 24 Hour Rule

The twenty-four-hour rule suggests that you hold off on arguing, complaining, disagreeing, yelling, or fighting with your spouse for at least twenty-four hours after sensing a potential conflict. I know what you're thinking: if you wait twenty-four hours, you might forget what the issue was. Exactly—that's the idea! Most marital arguments are minor and, with a little time, reveal themselves to be unworthy of serious conflict. What may seem significant in the heat of the moment often fades when you take a step back. Keeping this perspective helps you stay focused on what truly matters—your relationship as a whole.

Finances are a frequent challenge for married couples. While money is often cited as the second leading cause of divorce, it might actually be the top reason couples argue. One way to prevent money from becoming a recurring source of conflict is to accept the idea of a "marriage tax." This means understanding that a portion of your income will go toward purchases your spouse makes that you may not personally value.

If you believe something is a waste of money, chances are your spouse may feel differently—and that's where disagreements can start. This challenge is a natural part of any marriage and is not exclusive to those with limited finances; even wealthy couples can find themselves at odds over spending.

One area where I often notice unnecessary spending is on soaps: shampoos, conditioners, dish soap, hand soap, and so on. When I check my kids' showers, there are often a dozen half-used bottles of shampoo, conditioner, and body wash. Under the kitchen sink? It's filled with multiple hand soaps and specialized kitchen soaps. How many different kinds of soap does anyone actually need? Will using tea tree oil soap really make you smell better? Isn't tea tree oil just a fancy term for tree sap? If we're telling kids to shower after climbing trees, why would we then ask them to wash with a soap that's derived from those same trees? They might as well scrub down with the sap while they're up there!

Soaps now have so many ingredients that entire stores are dedicated to selling just soap! Who would have imagined that? From beeswax and palm oil to cocoa and shea butter, companies are constantly adding new elements to appeal to buyers.

When I travel, I just grab any soap and use it for both my hair and body—simple and effective! At this rate, though, it wouldn't surprise me if marketers started targeting specific body parts with their products. Soon enough, we'll be seeing foot conditioner and varieties of exfoliating cream for the earlobe.

I think fancy soaps are a waste of money, but my wife disagrees. So, I tell myself that my "tax bracket" is just a little higher now, even if only in my head, and that extra money goes towards buying organic soap berries picked by free-range monkeys. While I'm not thrilled about the cost of overpriced soaps, I choose to see it as a small tax for a happy wife and marriage. Plus, I'm doing my part to keep monkeys gainfully employed!

Understand that not every dollar you earn will be spent wisely. When money becomes a source of tension, consider it just another tax. This shift in perspective can save you a lot of frustration and help maintain harmony in your relationship.

If you are married, consider the last argument you had with your spouse. Can you remember what it was about, even if it was just a month ago? Most people struggle to recall such disputes, and for good reason: they often stem from trivial issues that fade from memory. When you think back, it's likely that the arguments were not significant enough to warrant long-term remembrance.

Interestingly, if you had a similar disagreement with a friend, you probably wouldn't feel as upset. Why? Because the emotional connection you share with your spouse is deeper, amplifying the weight of any conflict. As I reflect on my own experiences for this book, I find it challenging to pinpoint specific arguments I've had with my wife. It's not that we haven't disagreed; it's just that those conflicts were likely so inconsequential that they'd be embarrassing to even mention now.

If you can recall a specific argument with your spouse, it may indicate that you're holding onto a grudge. This can be detrimental to your mental well-being, as resentment can weigh heavily on you over time. The longer you keep those negative feelings bottled up, the more they can fester, leading to greater emotional pain and distance in your relationship. Letting go of grudges is essential for maintaining a healthy relationship.

Imagine a high school professor who extends his arm straight out holding up a glass of water and asks his students to guess its weight. Some estimate it at six ounces, while others guess ten. The teacher then explains that the actual weight is irrelevant; what truly matters is how long you hold the glass with your arm extended. If you support it for just a minute, it feels almost weightless. However, after an hour, it starts to strain your arm, and by the end of a day, your arm may be in severe pain. The weight itself hasn't changed; it's the prolonged effort of holding onto it that has intensified the pain.

Life operates in much the same way. When we cling to grudges and refuse to let go, the emotional burden can become unbearably heavy. Don't allow resentment to sabotage your marriage or cloud your happiness. Letting go is a vital step toward a thriving relationship.

Emotional arguments, by their very nature, are often unproductive. When one or both spouses are caught up in their feelings, meaningful communication becomes nearly impossible. I learned this valuable lesson while raising my children.

Can children become emotional? Absolutely! The challenge arises when they're in that heightened emotional state; it's simply not possible to reason with them. Instead, it's best to wait until they've calmed down, allowing some rationality to return. If they happen to be teenagers, then you may have to wait a few days, or maybe even years.

Some psychologists have described teenagers as having symptoms similar to brain damage until they reach their early twenties. If you have ever lived through that time period, you can attest to what scientists are talking about.

When raising children, you don't have to win every battle, and you must pick which ones are worth fighting over. With your spouse, you don't need to win *any* battles. It is imperative that you are able to discuss issues as calm, rational people, and that means taking emotion out of the equation. And once you wait 24 hours and have calmed down, you will see that what you were fighting about is probably meaningless.

There are issues in a marriage where you may never agree with your spouse. This does not need to get in the way of an amazing marriage. This manifested itself recently when President Donald Trump was in his first term of office. I know of a marriage where this became such an emotional issue that it ended up in divorce.

Don't Let Politics Trump Your Marriage

D id Donald Trump's first presidency really cause numerous divorces? More likely, it served as a trigger that intensified issues already present in strained relationships.

A study by Wakefield Research, titled The Trump Effect on American Relationships, found that 29% of Americans in relationships or marriages acknowledged experiencing tension with their spouse due to the political climate under President Trump in his first term. Additionally, 22% reported knowing a couple whose marriage or relationship was negatively affected during his time in office.

A report from the Michigan Institute for Fighting Family Education revealed that during Donald Trump's presidency, political conflicts became the leading factor in divorces among American couples. His tenure also sparked more family discord than any recent economic or social factor, leading to a notable rise in heated arguments, family disownments, and even relatives being removed from wills.

Dr. Philip Rangle, who led the study, observed, "Nobody is neutral about Donald Trump. If couples aren't aligned in their views on him, it often spells trouble. 'Divorce by Trump,' as we now call it, has become so widespread that it surpasses the big three factors — financial stress, religious differences, and infidelity — as a leading cause of breakups."

Case study: An acquaintance told me about the strain in his relationship with his wife during President Trumps first term. He was a Republican and she worked for an organization aligned with the Democratic Party. The marriage could have survived, but his wife was highly anti-Trump. During family gatherings such as Thanksgiving, she would talk incessantly about how much she hated him. This caused contempt in the marriage and it ended up in divorce.

How can couples navigate such deep political divides in their relationship? If one spouse is an ardent supporter and the other is vehemently opposed, the best strategy is often to make the topic off-limits. If a spouse feels compelled to constantly voice their opinion, it's essential to have a candid discussion about the impact this can have on your relationship. Explain that continually bringing up polarizing views strains your bond and could even harm your marriage. Agreeing to disagree, with a mutual understanding to keep politics out of your personal space, can help preserve the marriage.

Is this the best approach? When it comes to our loved ones, we should prioritize actions that bring us closer together. If this means making certain topics off-limits at home, then it's a necessary step to protect the relationship.

This same principle applies in marriage. Communicating with your spouse when emotions are high is like trading stocks based when you are emotional—you're likely to lose. But here, it's not money at stake; it's the depth of your relationship. If you wait twenty-four hours before bringing up a disagreement, you're more likely to approach it calmly and see that the issue wasn't as significant as it first seemed. But when it comes to elections, it's sometimes better to make it an off topic subject and just agree to disagree so you Don't Let Politics Trump Your Marriage.

Think Before You Speak

The most valuable advice I can give anyone in a committed relationship is to think before you speak. This has been instrumental in my 23+ years of marriage with minimal conflict. When I do slip up, I have enough goodwill built up that my wife lets it go without staying upset. But when you're dating, one careless comment can end a relationship, potentially costing you an amazing lifelong partner. So, remember: thoughtful words can make all the difference.

Once words are spoken, they're out there—you can't take them back. Even with an apology, those words linger, and your spouse may always remember that they came from you. A solid rule of thumb in relationships, and in life, is: if it isn't positive or constructive, don't say it.

There's a parable about a student who constantly speaks poorly of others. The teacher instructs the student to take a pillow to the roof, rip it open, and scatter the feathers into the wind. The next day, the student returns and says he completed the task. The teacher then tells him to go collect every feather. The student, surprised, replies that it's impossible—they've scattered across the city. The teacher explains that this is exactly what happens when we speak negatively about others. Once released, those words spread far and wide, beyond our control, and the damage can be irreparable.

Have you ever seen a courtroom scene where an attorney asks a damaging or incriminating question, and the judge quickly says, "Strike that from the record"? The judge is instructing the jury to disregard the statement, but once words are spoken, they linger in memory. A skilled attorney knows this well and may even anticipate the judge's objection. But by putting those words out there, the attorney plants a seed in the jurors' minds that can't easily be erased, often with the aim of influencing the case in his favor.

The same principle applies in dating and marriage. Even if you spoke in a moment of emotion, even if you apologized and explained that the hurtful things you said were said in anger, those words linger in your spouse's memory. So be mindful of what you say, and always think before you speak!

It's usually best to stay quiet when you're feeling emotional. Acting or speaking in an emotional state rarely leads to positive outcomes. The words "hate" and "divorce" should not be part of your vernacular.

You probably grew up hearing, "Sticks and stones may break my bones, but words will never hurt me." This couldn't be further from the truth. Words do hurt, especially in close relationships. When a neighborhood kid said something mean, it was easy to shrug off because there was no deep emotional connection. But when a spouse says something hurtful, it can linger for years due to that strong bond. So when should you think before you speak? Every single time.

Here's a simple acronym to help you pause and think before speaking, especially when emotions are high. This practice can prevent hurtful words and lead to a healthier, more fulfilling relationship. The acronym is *THINK*.

T stands for True. One of the strongest ways to build trust in your relationship is by ensuring that what you say is truthful and that your actions align with your words. Always aim for honesty with your spouse, but this goes beyond simply telling the truth—it means being reliable. If you say you'll do something, follow through.

This includes even the small things, like a husband saying he'll take the trash out that night. When he doesn't follow through, it may seem minor, but each unfulfilled promise plants small seeds of doubt in his spouse's mind. Once or twice might not matter, but if it becomes a pattern, these little disappointments can erode trust over time.

The husband might think it's no big deal to take the trash out in the morning before the trash collectors arrive instead of at night as promised. To him, the end result is the same—the chore gets done. But that's not the real issue. If you say you'll do something at a certain time and then don't, it subtly chips away at trust, regardless of the importance. Some readers may disagree with this level of commitment to one's word, but this kind of consistency is what builds the strong foundation needed for a marriage to reach the 4th phase of Never Leaving.

It's like pulling a single thread from a sweater—one thread might not make a difference, but if you keep removing them one by one, eventually it won't be a sweater anymore. Similarly, if the words you speak gradually erode your spouse's trust, your marriage can slowly come apart, ending up like that unraveled sweater: a tangled pile with nothing to hold it together.

This is the opposite of what you want in a relationship. You want both of you to trust every word and action, building a connection so strong that you reach the point of Never Leaving.

H stands for Helpful. If your words aren't improving the situation, they're better left unsaid. In a disagreement with your spouse, the goal should be to speak in ways that promotes peace. Prioritizing peace in your home should be the mantra you live by—it's essential for a strong marriage.

I stands for Important. Ask yourself if what you're saying truly matters in this moment, or if you're speaking just to be heard or to feel like you "won" the argument. If it's not genuinely important, it may be better left unsaid.

N stands for Necessary. Speak only what's essential to foster peace in your relationship. Early in my marriage, I often thought certain things were necessary to say, only to realize that I hadn't fully considered my spouse's perspective. Focus on what's truly needed to support harmony and understanding between you and your spouse.

K stands for Kind. Whatever you say to your spouse should come from a place of kindness. This is one of the cornerstones of a strong and fulfilling marriage. Kind words build up, while harsh ones tear down. In our home, our guiding mantra is "compliment, don't criticize." A foundation of supportive communication will lead to a happier marriage.

There's a valuable skill that can help you communicate with your spouse in a way that minimizes conflict. Psychologist Robert Sternberg calls it practical intelligence, one of three types of intelligence he identifies (the other two being analytical and creative). While analytical and creative intelligence are largely innate, practical intelligence is a skill you can develop. It's about knowing when and how to say things, understanding the nuances of situations, and responding thoughtfully. This type of intelligence helps you read situations accurately, allowing for more harmonious interactions with your spouse.

Spouses involved in a great marriage have the social savviness to understand what they should and shouldn't say to each other. There is a *right* way to say something, a *right* time to say something, and the right *person* to say something. Sometimes you are not the right person to say something to your spouse. It's possible that your spouse will more likely listen to a friend or a co-worker. It's just part of the nuances of communication.

I know from personal experience that there are things my wife wants me to do and I will not do it if it's coming from her. It's only when I hear it from *someone else, then I'll decide to do it.* This is not a conscious decision that we make in our heads that we will listen to some people and not listen to others. It's just hard for us to internalize things we hear from people that are close to us.

Learning to think before you speak will keep you from sleeping in the doghouse and will get you closer to Never Leaving!

SLIM:
Sometimes Less is More

This acronym can have implications across various aspects of life, but there's one specific area where embracing "less" can lead to "more"—specifically, a more passionate marriage. By minimizing the number of external problems you bring into your relationship, you can enhance the concept of *SLIM*. Often, these challenges stem from work or health issues. While it's natural to lean on your spouse for support, consider whether discussing certain topics is necessary. Avoiding unnecessary stress or pressure can create a more harmonious environment, allowing your relationship to flourish without the weight of outside burdens.

For instance, imagine you've just lost a significant business deal for various reasons. You don't need to burden your spouse with every detail of the situation. Instead, you could simply share that you lost the sale and plan to learn from the experience moving forward. If your spouse works in the same field, they might be interested in more specifics, but that's not the norm. It's important to remember that being married doesn't automatically mean your spouse wants to hear every aspect of your day. Filtering your conversations can help maintain a positive atmosphere and keep the focus on what truly matters.

During my time in business, whenever I closed a profitable deal, I would feel an urge to rush home and share my excitement with my wife. However, after a few years, I noticed that her enthusiasm for my work began to wane. It's not uncommon for one spouse to lose interest in the other's career over time, especially if you have been married for many years. Do not confuse your spouse's interest in your work with the success of your marriage. Your work should be what you do to pay the bills. It should not define you as a person.

If you work in a high-stress environment, like a hospital, your spouse may not want to hear every detail of your day, especially if it was challenging. Instead of diving into specifics about a rough day, it's often better to simply acknowledge that it was tough. A helpful guideline is to keep your conversations positive—if something isn't uplifting or necessary to share, consider holding back. When your spouse knows that your discussions will revolve around positive or joyful experiences, they'll be more eager to engage with you. Conversely, if your conversations are dominated by negativity, they might begin to associate you with those feelings, which can create distance in the relationship. Think about how you feel when interacting with someone who is consistently a downer; chances are, you don't look forward to those conversations.

I encountered a personal situation that truly highlighted the importance of maintaining a positive outlook. When I was diagnosed with lung cancer at the age of forty-seven, it came just two months after my wife had given birth to our youngest child. At that time, we were also parenting four other children, all aged seven and under. This was undeniably a stressful period for our family.

Staying positive was crucial. If I had allowed negativity to take over, our already challenging circumstances could have escalated into something worse. By focusing on hope, I not only supported my own mental health, but also created an environment where my family could cope more effectively with the stress we were facing. This experience reinforced for me the significance of positivity in the face of adversity, particularly within a marriage.

Since my wife was already having to go through a lot after having a baby, I had to be careful about what I told her about my condition. I did not want to stress her out more than she needed to be. I definitely kept her informed of what was happening, but I did not have to let her know *everything*.

The doctor told me things my wife didn't need to hear such as the extremely high death rate for lung cancer. That would not have accomplished anything except cause unnecessary stress. Although she was there when I needed to talk to her, I filtered what I told her.

Your home should be a sanctuary filled with love, happiness, and positivity. Allowing negativity from external sources can disrupt the environment essential for a thriving marriage. Sometimes saying less to your spouse will bring more passion to your relationship. Making sure your spouse is happy, will ensure that you are happy, and sometime less is more when it comes to how you communicate with your spouse.

Final
Blessing

I hope you enjoyed reading this book! Marriage is one of life's most beautiful and meaningful relationships. While saying 'I do' may be easy, nurturing love and keeping it strong requires consistent effort. Think of it like sunscreen: every time you compliment your spouse, you're applying a protective layer that keeps your relationship thriving. However, every criticism wipes that sunscreen away—and no amount of aloe vera can soothe the sting of a relationship that's been burned. So, keep reapplying the sunscreen, and enjoy a lifetime of love, happiness, and harmony.

My heartfelt blessing for all my readers is that you find a partner to love for a lifetime—not just in a good or even great marriage, but in an extraordinary one. May you reach the pinnacle of Never Leaving, where your relationship is filled with joy, passion, and an unshakable commitment to one another.

If you enjoyed my book or have constructive feedback, I would truly appreciate it if you left a review on Amazon.

Your thoughts mean a lot to me! Don't forget to check out The Coach Ratner Podcast, where you can listen to many of my books as free audiobooks. You can also download many of my books for free at coachratner.com. Thank you for taking the time to read this book—I'm deeply grateful for your support!

About
The Author

Coach Ratner was a world-class rare coin dealer & real estate developer in America. He has now transitioned himself into an influential educator for organizations who seek inspiration. His focus is on fostering meaningful relationships, building self-esteem, and providing spiritual motivation.

The Coach Ratner Podcast is available on
YouTube, Spotify, Apple
and wherever you listen to your favorite podcasts.

To book Coach Ratner, you can reach him at
CoachRatner@gmail.com.

For those of you who want to get up close
and personal, you can find him weekly at the
Aish Essentials program
in the Old City of Jerusalem,
or at **www.CoachRatner.com**.

Preview for

Never Feel
Unloved Again:

Symptoms & Strategies
to Cure Low Self-Esteem

Start Here

**"The greatest prison we can put ourselves in
is worrying about what other people think of us."**

In 2021, the Centers for Disease, Control & Prevention, also known as the CDC, released a staggering report that one out of every three teenage girls had seriously contemplated committing suicide. This is based on interviews from 17,000 teenagers. The rate for boys is half of that, which is interesting in the way that they published the report. You could understand this report to mean that the rate for boys contemplating suicide implies acceptability, or downplays its significance.

Imagine teaching a classroom of 30 teenage boys and finding out that five of them are thinking about suicide. You would think there is something in the water or air that is poisoning them. This still represents an alarmingly high number that warrants attention.

For high schoolers that have actually attempted suicide and not just thought about it, the numbers are astounding. Ten-percent of youth in grades 9-12 reported that they had made at least one suicide attempt in the past 12 months.[6] I don't know about you, but these numbers are even hard to grasp.

The prevalence of this issue has reached epidemic proportions. While it's crucial to recognize that not all instances of suicide attempts or contemplation stem solely from low self-esteem, addressing the root of the problem is imperative. Encouraging individuals to cultivate self-love could significantly alter the landscape. The alarming surge in the usage of antidepressants serves as a stark reminder of the severity of this crisis.

I don't know anyone that has not gone through periods of life where they have had low self-esteem, but not to the extent we are seeing today.

When does the issue with low self-esteem start? Usually it occurs during and after puberty and can persist until our twenties and beyond. For many, it's when their mother asked them to put on a wool winter hat before going outside on a frigid winter morning. Most of us have no problem doing it in 3rd or 4th grade. However, a shift occurs as self-consciousness settles in. Wearing a wool winter hat to the bus stop suddenly feels awkward, and creates a fear of appearing socially undesirable in the eyes of your peers. Looking like what we think is a geek in front of students of the opposite gender is then outweighed by the discomfort of freezing our ears off.

The greatest prison we can put ourselves in is worrying about what other people think of us. This can be one of the most limiting and suffocating experiences in life. When we become preoccupied with seeking external validation and approval, we allow the opinions of others to define our

---

6   According to the American Foundation for Suicide Prevention, based on the most recent Youth Risk Behaviors Survey from 2021

self-worth and happiness. If we don't get those opinions that give us that validation, then this can lead to a cycle of anxiety, unhappiness, and of course, low self-esteem. Freeing ourselves from this mental prison involves a journey of self-discovery and acceptance.

Our hope is that we will outgrow the feeling of low self-esteem and we will eventually be happy with ourselves, paving the way for self-love. Regrettably, this hope does not materialize for many. Because of that, the struggle with low self-esteem continues into our adult life. No one wants to have the feeling of being unloved, by others or by yourself. If you don't love yourself, it will be a difficult task to love others.

I have navigated through phases of low self-esteem in various stages of my life. Unfortunately, for a long time, I did not have the clarity to seek help or educate myself about it to overcome these struggles. Now that I do have clarity, I want to turn my mess into my message.

"I want to turn my mess into my message"

For those grappling with low self-esteem, my aim is that by the time you reach the end of this book, you'll find yourself on the path towards building positive self-esteem. If you're fortunate enough not to battle with low self-esteem, I hope the insights within this book become a valuable resource in assisting those around you who may be struggling. Additionally, if you're dealing with clinical depression, consider using this book as a supplement to therapy and medication, working together towards a journey of happiness and joy.

Low self-esteem is not something that the Social Security Administration considers a disability. It does not fit into their criteria for financial assistance like they do with other disabilities. However, the long-term problem with low self-esteem is that it has the potential to manifest itself as a physical ailment. The correlation between emotional well-being and physical health is reflected in that the happiest people tend to live the longest lives. Our emotional and physical states are intricately connected and can have a profound impact on our overall health.

Low self-esteem is somewhat similar to darkness. Darkness does not exist. It is just an absence of light. Even the early narrative of the Bible starts with "darkness upon the surface of the deep" right before the famous words, "...and let there be light." It is obvious that darkness was there before creation and the Bible even tells us that. How could anything have existed before creation? It didn't, because it does not exist. Darkness is just an absence of light. Black is not a color. Which means, any low self-esteem that someone has, in theory, does not exist. It is just an absence of light that has permeated the life of someone with low self-esteem. However, try telling that to someone with low-self-esteem and they will probably throw a soda can at your head.

If low self-esteem does not exist, you may need to change the vision of how you see yourself. By altering your mindset, you have the power to transform your entire life. Your city of happiness only resides in one place; your state of mind. If you can change your mindset, you can change your life.

"Your city of happiness only resides in one place; your state of mind"

The ultimate goal of this book is to bring light back into your life. Much like a small candle can light up an entire dark room, I hope that this book will serve as the spark that brightens up your soul, guiding you out of the dark place that you may find yourself in. Ultimately, I will unveil my 12 strategies that will infuse light back into your life. If you are not happier after reading this book than when you started, then I have failed, and I have no intention of failing. Your well-being is the driving force behind every word. I am not writing this book for anything or anyone else, but to help you.

You may look at yourself just like a raw diamond: rough around the edges, maybe a bit oddly shaped, full of irregularities and imperfections. A raw diamond that is transformed through precise cutting, with the correct angles, shape and size, is one of the most beautiful objects in the world. Its beauty is based on its ability to allow light to permeate it and reflect its brilliance back out.

You are just like a diamond in the rough brimming with untapped potential. All that is required is careful reshaping of your mindset to allow the light to permeate your soul. What is exciting is that you may be the most beautiful diamond in the world, but your low self-esteem is hiding your inner brilliance. When you finally overcome your low self-esteem, you will recognize the dazzling person that you are. You will then spread that brilliance back out to the world and discover that there are *many* people who love you. You will then *Never Feel Unloved Again.*

The Symptoms of Low Self-Esteem

This chapter aims to highlight symptoms that may be indicative of having low self-esteem. It does not mean that experiencing any of these symptoms conclusively indicates a struggle with low self-esteem. Just like having a cough and sore throat doesn't necessarily mean you have COVID-19—it could be a common cold, strep throat, or another ailment. These clues are just indicators that you may be dealing with the potential of having it.

If you find yourself resonating with several of these traits, there's no cause for panic. Many individuals encounter these challenges at different points in their lives. Understanding these symptoms is crucial for your emotional well-being. Awareness will help you navigate these feelings, cultivating a greater understanding of what you need to do to maintain happiness in your life.

1. Imposter Syndrome

This is when you doubt your skills, talents, and accomplishments and you have a fear of being exposed as a fraud. It affects individuals across various stages of their careers and expertise levels. The term "syndrome" can sometimes imply a more severe or clinical condition, but imposter syndrome is not a mental disorder; rather, it is a psychological pattern of self-doubt and fear of being exposed as a fraud, despite evidence of competence.

This syndrome is not relevant for someone who is just in the beginning of a new path in life, because you may really be a bit of an imposter. The syndrome of being an imposter is relevant for someone who is just average in their skill level, or someone who is at the top of their game, what you would call an expert in their field.

Comedians often grapple with the challenge of taking the stage, wondering if the audience will think their material is funny. It's only once they hear genuine laughter from the audience that their self-assurance begins to resurface.

Courtroom attorneys may have doubt in presenting arguments before a judge. Their confidence may waver initially, but as they present their case, their self-assurance tends to strengthen.

It also may be the rookie quarterback who was a star in college and now struggles in the professional league. They may be an excellent quarterback, but the intensely higher speed of the professional game versus college is too much for them. The combination of imposter syndrome and the quickness of the game lends to the fact that few rookies are able to reach their potential. It is also one of the reasons that so few rookie quarterbacks can start in the National Football League, or why evaluators of talent have such a difficult time drafting successful quarterbacks.

It may be a female model who feels like she is ugly and does not like herself. If you think back to your high school days, you might recall a girl that was considered beautiful, yet never acknowledged your existence or of anyone else in your social circle. Although she was always called "stuck-up", she might have been exceptionally shy or struggled with low self-esteem. Your perception of her beauty likely shaped assumptions about her confidence, whereas if she were merely average-looking, you might not have labeled her as stuck-up and probably would never have given her a moment of your thoughts.

It may be you, who's an expert in something, but you may even struggle to gain confidence because you think you may be a fake. It is only when you have done something over and over for many years, when you feel confident that you are not a phony. It is when you have positive self-esteem that you clearly recognize that you know what you are doing, without feeling that you are an imposter.

Occasionally, experiencing a touch of imposter syndrome can be a catalyst for achieving skills beyond comprehension even if they are considered at the pinnacle of one's field. There's a compelling argument that suggests this is essential for those regarded as the greatest of all time.

Despite Tom Brady getting his fifth Super Bowl victory, which sealed his legacy as the GOAT, the Greatest Of All Time, he may have grappled with imposter syndrome. This sense of self-doubt could have propelled him to elevate his game to unprecedented levels, defying age norms and securing a remarkable 6th and 7th Super Bowl ring, a feat once deemed unattainable.

Michael Jordan consistently faced challenges throughout his career, starting from the disappointment of being cut from the varsity high school basketball team to being labeled a below-average defender after his rookie year in the NBA.

Whether you label it a "chip on the shoulder" or a touch of "imposter syndrome," that motivating factor propelled

Michael Jordan to relentlessly practice, ultimately leading him to become not only the greatest basketball player in history, but the best defender the game has ever seen. Which may irk some people because without the defender status, he would still be considered the GOAT.

Imposter syndrome tends to be the most damaging when you find yourself in the middle of the talent spectrum. It's often when you're merely average in a particular area that imposter syndrome can negatively impact your self-esteem.

Here are five tools to get over imposter syndrome:

1. Set realistic goals because you don't have to accomplish everything all at once. The race to the finish line isn't won by the first person out of the gate. It is slow, steady, consistent work that will improve your talents and skills. If you're a rookie in anything, you'll have to slowly get over imposter syndrome. If you are average as far as talent, set realistic goals and you won't have to deal with imposter syndrome. If you are a superstar already, use the imposter syndrome you feel to get even better and to surpass what may be already recognized as great. You are already an outlier, so don't let it bother you too much.

2. Define what success means to you, because if you don't, someone else will do it for you. Then you may have been successful in life and completely missed it. This will help you avoid imposter syndrome.

3. Stay away from toxic competitions where winning is so important. Michael Jordan only won 6 championships out of 15 seasons. Were those other 9 seasons a failure? Of course not! You will *not* win most of the time, so don't feel like an imposter if you don't win or are not #1 in your field.

4. Don't rely exclusively on external validation for your self-esteem. Have confidence that you are an expert in what you are doing, even if no one else recognizes it.

5. Don't let your job define who you are as a person, unless your job is so meaningful beyond the financial reward that you want it to define you. Set limits and boundaries to avoid overworking. Maybe you feel like you are not qualified for your job and feel that you are an imposter. Understand that this is just how you make a living, not the person you are to your friends, family, and loved ones. Your job should define what you do for a living, not who you are.

One should refrain from boasting about personal achievements and attribute success to others whenever feasible. This concept reflects the virtue of humility. Practicing humility serves as a powerful antidote to imposter syndrome, fostering an awareness that one's skills and talents are bestowed gifts that one utilizes to the best of their ability.

Picture a scenario where a member of an elementary school PTA single-handedly puts together a highly successful fundraiser. Instead of taking all the credit, she praises the other board members, despite them doing very little. This act of humility involves reducing the focus on herself and acknowledging the efforts of others. Someone with the highest levels of self-esteem does not worry about receiving accolades, rather, their humility signifies a mindset that allows one to share credit without seeking recognition. Being humble is not thinking less of yourself, but thinking less *about* yourself.

"Being humble is not thinking less of yourself, but thinking less about yourself"

When one has strong self-esteem, the need to claim the credit diminishes, and a willingness to share the honor will increase. Even when everyone knows that the project succeeded because of one person, individuals with strong self-esteem opt to distribute credit, potentially inspiring others to take on more responsibilities in the future. With this in mind, recognizing imposter syndrome as a symptom of low self-esteem, one can learn to deflect praise and realize that any feeling of being a "fake" is not justified.

Avoiding Social Interaction

Can you recall a student in college who always stayed in their dorm, even on weekends, while you were out going to bars and parties? You might have perceived them to be boring. However, one factor to consider is that they may be an introvert, finding joy in solitary activities like reading or studying. Their definition of fun simply differed from your definition of fun. This does not necessarily indicate low self-esteem; rather, it reflects on their preference in how they derive satisfaction; reading a book in their dorm room on a weekend is fun for them, even though it may not be fun for you.

There is a fine line between someone who avoids social situations because they are an introvert, versus someone who doesn't like being in social situations, because *they are scared out of their minds!* The latter may have anxiety and have a constant fear of being judged. These individuals may think they are ugly or unworthy of conversation; plagued by fears that deter them from going into any social interaction.

Sometimes, individuals might label themselves as introverts when, in fact, their avoidance of social situations stems from low self-esteem. This may manifest itself in a reluctance to engage with others, driven by their belief that they are not capable to be loved, or able to be loved by someone else. In this scenario, making excuses to avoid social interactions becomes a way of sidestepping their deeper issue and their self-imposed introvert label is being used as a protection from facing their reality.

This is similar to some individuals who may claim they don't want to get married, not because they have no interest in marriage, but because…

Now available

on Amazon